Praise for Becomin~ ~~~~~

In a culture plagued with self-doubt and distraction, Stephanie's book is a welcome voice, gently bringing us back to our true nature, helping us to redefine what true strength, power and fierceness really is; pointing us inward where we can find qualities that we forgot we were endowed with and helping us remember the deep meaning and purpose in our lives that can bring us true joy.

Tarek Mounib
Filmmaker/Producer *Free Trip to Egypt*,
Founder of Kindness Films

In *Becoming Fierce,* Stephanie James brilliantly teaches us how to transform our deepest challenges, grief, and pain into the greatest gifts we have to offer to the world. If you have ever longed to find your purpose and true power, this amazing, transformative book will lovingly guide you, step by step, into a bold, beautiful, and deeply meaningful life.

Laura Davis
Author, *The Courage to Heal* and *The Burning Light of Two Stars*

A gentle and provocative book, stimulating considerable thought, and igniting the heart space while providing the practical insights to build the inner strength and courage to overcome. *Becoming Fierce* is an astonishing revelation of balance, poignancy, and meaning. Stephanie James has captured beautifully the essence of universal wisdom and self-love.

Pauline Nguyen
International Speaker, Award Winning Author,
Spiritual Entrepreneur

Becoming Fierce is a beautiful blend of personal stories from Stephanie's own ignited path along with active journaling prompts, guidance, and exploration that allows the reader to uncover their own authentic fierceness. It is the perfect book for anyone on the awakened path who is desiring to go deeper into greater states of self-love, wholeness and thriving. I Love Stephanie, and I Love seeing her more than thirty years of assisting humans in their radiance shared in this brilliant book!

Dr. Heather Kristian Strang

Author of ten books including *Sacred Love in Sacred Times*, Host of *Awakening: The Podcast*

Stephanie James is a friend, sister, and spiritual warrior whose new book, *Becoming Fierce* takes us on a journey of authentic inquiry, discovery, and redemption. She is the skillful guide on this journey of open-hearted storytelling, revealing her best strategies from a thirty-year career in mental health. Straight from the heart, she brings us meaning, purpose, and the rewards of her career as a therapist and spiritual seeker, inviting us into our own personal therapy session. *Becoming Fierce* is fiercely provocative as we are guided gently, and skillfully to uncover the practiced techniques of becoming more whole and awake so that we have greater access to creating a bold and beautiful life.

Sedena Cappannelli

Award-winning co-author of *Do Not Go Quietly, A Guide to Living Consciously & Aging Wisely for People Who Weren't Born Yesterday,* presenter and co-producer of the *Ageless Living Television Series for PBS.*

All of us experience good times and times that can take us through the *dark night of the soul.* If we are fortunate, we discover that our most difficult experiences often catalyze our most profound growth. In *Becoming Fierce,* Stephanie James shares her life's journey and powerful discoveries about how our challenges can become the spark for creating a bold and beautiful life. This book will light up your life!

Jacob Israel Liberman

Author of *Luminous Life: How the Science of Light Unlocks the Art of living*

Stephanie James is a rare combination of warm heart, joyful spirit, and deep soul. When I first saw the word Fierce in the title, I thought she had written something about how to be Fierce, like a model on a runway, or a soldier on the battlefield. That is not it at all. Stephanie is talking about Fierce in the sense of being and feeling fully in your power and letting that truth out into our world. Instead of being shut down, constricted, or closed off, Stephanie talks about letting your Light shine fully, because we need *you* fully in today's world. Live fiercely, love fiercely, work fiercely, and let go of what does not serve you and others fiercely; and, yes, take care of yourself fiercely.

Martin Rutte
Founder www.ProjectHeavenOnEarth.com

Once again Stephanie James has captured lightning in a bottle with her brilliant new book. Like all her work, she stimulates the reader to expand and grow in what they believe is possible.

Paul Samuel Dolman
Host of the podcast *What Matters Most*

Stephanie James takes you into the raw, transformative experiences of life as she shares from her personal stories and those of luminaries she has interviewed during her career as a radio host. You see how true passion for one's journey is born— through the gritty challenges that come with being human. If you have ever wanted to know the secrets of awakening your potential, this is the book to read. Accept her invitation to discover how to become fierce enough to ignite your authentic self, and your life will be forever changed.

Misa Hopkins
Five times bestselling author of *The Root of All Healing* and the *Sacred Feminine Awakening* series

Becoming Fierce is a must read for all humans on a path of heart towards co-creating a life, and world of wholeness and beauty. Stephanie's authentic and unconditionally loving presence takes the reader on a journey of deep reflection and discovery. This book is a treasure trove, packed with both practical skill sets and sage wisdom to navigate the territory of life with courage, passion, and joy.

Gabriela Masala

Life Artist, Creative Catalyst

Stephanie James is a beautiful storyteller that really captures the heart of what it is to be human. This is a book that will move you, inspire you, and open your heart; it is something everyone should read.

Tom Cronin

Founder of The Stillness Project,
Filmmaker/Author of *The Portal*

Stephanie James has written a book that will not only inspire you but empower you to become fierce in your own life. Through wisdom, experience, and by sharing her own amazing journey, she shows us how healing and change are possible. Stephanie gives us hope that we too can create a fully ignited life where we fiercely love others, ourselves, and our lives.

Allison Carmen

Bestselling author of *The Gift of Maybe: Finding Hope and Possibility in Uncertain Times* and *A Year Without Men*

To Peter –

BECOMING
FIERCE

You are such a
bright light that

STEPHANIE JAMES

illuminates so many
hearts! Shine On!
♡, Stephanie

Edited by Laurie Knight

An Imprint for GracePoint Publishing (www.GracePointPublishing.com)

GracePoint Matrix, LLC
624 S. Cascade Ave, Suite 201
Colorado Springs, CO 80903
www.GracePointMatrix.com
Email: Admin@GracePointMatrix.com
SAN # 991-6032

A Library of Congress Control Number has been requested and is pending.

ISBN: (Paperback) 978-1-955272-34-6
eISBN: 978-1-955272-33-9

Books may be purchased for educational, business, or sales promotional
use. For bulk order requests and price schedule contact:
Orders@GracePointPublishing.com

FOREWORD

Damn, life can be hard!

I mean all you have to do is look at your phone, your TV, or your computer and the negativity relentlessly streams in— politics, war, conspiracy theories, all exaggerated by the pandemic. It's like a consistent layer of stress and anxiety is smothering us every day.

And that's just the outside world.

Our personal, internal world can be challenging too. Our negative self-talk seems to be second-guessing ourselves, beating ourselves up for not making better choices, or not living up to the distorted lives of others we see on social media. It's so exhausting; as if we're dragging through life wearing concrete boots.

How are you feeling through all this turmoil? Maybe you're numb and simply going through the motions. Maybe you feel defeated because every time you try to improve your life you just get knocked back down. Maybe you're on the edge of the proverbial springboard, bouncing up and down hesitant to leap into the next chapter of your life.

Whatever the reason is that brought you to this book, you can take a breath and relax. You're exactly where you need to be.

Stephanie James does an incredible job of explaining why we are at this point in our lives by sharing her own personal journey and accounts of clients she has worked with. She tells how the events and experiences we've been through shape our beliefs, behaviors, and the way we think. She explains how the stories we tell ourselves and others over and over again can keep us tethered to the past, not able to move confidently into our future, and she shows us why our brains have been wired to default to the worst-case scenario.

Honestly, being able to understand why you do the things you do is incredibly relieving, like a weight being lifted for the first time in your life.

Then she expertly guides you out of this frustration, not with "woo woo" crazy suggestions, but with practical, doable, easy to implement exercises that are so simple you could mistakenly think they couldn't possibly work. They include activities like journaling, breathing, dropping into your heart, playing, tapping into your intuition, gratitude, and more. See simple!

Now one of these things on their own may move the needle a little, but when you start to stack these life-changing nuggets, introducing them into your daily routine one at a time, get ready to start living life on a whole new level.

Imagine being able to remain grounded and calm regardless of what crazy stuff life throws at you or daring to dream a life so beautiful, rich, and fulfilling and knowing having everything you need to make it a reality. Imagine being in a supportive, passionate, and loving relationship, or having so much energy and vitality you are loving life to the fullest. What about using your time to make a contribution that fills you with pride and accomplishment?

Anything you put your mind to, you will be able to create because Stephanie gives you the blueprint.

Oh, and did I mention you'll be really happy and content?

What I know for sure is that, although we can't control the events that show up in our lives, we can control how we choose to see them, how we respond to them, and how long we allow them to affect us moving forward.

Each time we enter a new job or relationship we face new parts of ourselves that have been dormant and can only come to the surface when catalyzed by that new situation.

Even the stories we tell about the darkest moments of our lives can be reframed to inspire and help us grow.

All you need to do is apply what you learn here in this book and your life will be transformed. You will move through these kinds of situations with ease and grace. You'll be living life in technicolor, and the struggles of the past will stay in the past.

Now is the time to be fierce. Not the aggressive version but the fierceness of knowing you can positively influence the outcomes in your life and positively influence the people you love and serve.

Come on, let's do this.

Natalie Ledwell

Bestselling Author and Founder of Mind Movies

To my mother, who has been the most profound example of what it means to show up fierce in this world—never giving up, never losing faith, and continuing to love others unconditionally despite whatever challenges or hardships she has faced. Her ability to love and her complete devotion to her family, friends, community, and world has been an inspirational beacon that has illuminated my way through this life and a torch I will carry with me forever.

Table of Contents

BEGINNINGS

I live in Colorado. The weather can be unpredictable. One day, 70 degrees and the next, we have twelve inches of snow. The joke in Colorado is, "If you don't like the weather, wait fifteen minutes and it will change." Such a great metaphor for life. Always changing and unpredictable, indeed.

Every morning, regardless of the weather, I walk outside barefoot with my dog, put my feet on the earth, and soak up the sky and the sounds of the singing birds welcoming me to the day.

This grounds me to a deeper rhythm inside of myself, one where my heart aligns with the divine music that is always in full orchestra around us and in us if we stop to listen. It is the sound of life itself. It reminds me that no matter what the outer circumstances of my life may be, I can focus on what nourishes and strengthens me and connects deeply with the divine, as I stand in awe holding the beauty of it all.

This book is a calling card to your very soul. The reason that you are reading it is that you are ready to answer that call. You are ready to step into your inner life and begin to transmute, transcend, transform, and awaken the expanded version of yourself, your passion, and your fully-ignited purpose on this planet.

We live in an often challenging, and at times, very unpredictable world. We all face the experience of loss, pain, and difficulties throughout our lives. What if those exact experiences were actually the match point that ignited something within you that then became your gift to the world?

There is so much evolving and changing on the planet right now, and it can feel very overwhelming if you are gauging your well-being on the state of the world. Having just gone through our first worldwide pandemic, many people live in fear of what else could happen, and their sense of safety has been badly shaken. It is time for us to better understand this universal lesson that literally forced us to go inside and within. This time is an opportunity for each one of us to do the essential inner work that will help to not only transform and heal our own lives but will also help to heal humanity.

Life is inviting us to stop focusing on everything that is going on outside of us, to stop believing the fear narrative, and to let go of all the things that distract us from cultivating the resilience, joy, and grit it takes to live a bold, beautiful, and deeply meaningful life. We can let go of the focus on the outer world dictating our sense of well-being. The point of power is in the present moment. You get to choose what you want to focus on. This is an inside job and the time to begin is now. It is time to become fierce.

INTRODUCTION

Fierce /firs/:
showing a powerful and heartfelt intensity

Unlike what some people may think of when they hear the word fierce, my use of the word in this book is not about being mean, aggressive, or violent. Being fierce is all about the other synonyms associated with the word: powerful, strong, forceful, passionate, and fiery. It is about living a life out loud, full out, and embodying the beautiful, authentic expression that is you!

How do you fully ignite that spark? This book is a guidepost to help you on your journey, a roadmap to guide you down the paths that all lead back to your essential self and to the magnificent essence you were born with to shine, exude, and share with the world.

During our journey together we will be exploring the spark (your essence) and how to excavate any of its radiance that has been covered up by old limiting beliefs and difficult life circumstances. Don Miguel Ruiz said that we were all born wild and that we become domesticated as children, giving up our voices and the things that truly light us up in order to fit in and win approval from the adults in our lives (who ironically, have also given up their true wild nature and are not living fully authentic lives themselves).

You will learn how to identify, change, and rescript limiting beliefs that have kept you from truly accessing a life that is a full expression of who you were meant to be in this world. You will also realize why you have been born at a particular place, during this exact time, with absolute purpose on this planet. What if you were able to actualize an unlimited version of yourself? What if you discovered that it was your own limiting beliefs keeping you from living the life you most desired to live and that it had little to do with your outer circumstances? There are practices and processes that we will go through together to help you create a belief system that supports you in ascending to your highest expression of yourself.

I also share my story here. Yes, it is true: no one gets out of childhood unscathed, and mine is no exception. I hope my life will be an example of how you can face the most difficult of times, transcend them, and in the process, totally find your voice, your power, and your divine connection to Source which guides it all. I want you to find your own internal guidance system that you can rely on to help navigate through the storms of life and safely guide you back to shore. Through over fifty years of life experience, thirty years in the mental health and personal development field, an expanded career as a radio show and podcast host, filmmaker, producer, transformational life coach, and professional speaker, I have had the amazing blessing to live this expanded version of myself after playing small for decades! I am here to guide you into what it takes to create this bold and beautiful life and how to show up for yourself in new and amazing ways.

Finding your inner and outer voice, how to dig deep and discover what truly lights you up and inspires you, and how to keep your inner fire truly aflame are just some of the ways we will journey together through this book. We will discuss how finding your inner roar is one of the true keys to becoming fierce and living a life by your design. We will map the ways that surrender and serendipity play huge roles in navigating your life and open you to the divine wisdom that is always available. As you continue this journey you will find out how to cultivate joy, grit, and resilience and make them the cornerstones of the foundation that fully supports you. By utilizing the Take a Moment sections at the end of each chapter, you will learn how to use meditation, exercise, daily practice, and prosperity mindsets to create the life you have been longing to live—a life where you live fiercely and fully embodied.

As I write this, I am aware that each one of us holds the flame to ignite our best life. I have witnessed hundreds and hundreds of people healing throughout my career and have observed what tools and techniques worked for them and what left them stuck and unable to break through to a fierce life. I have had the profound privilege of interviewing the most brilliant minds and serving hearts on the planet: Mark Nepo, Bruce Lipton, Larry Dossey, Pedram Shojai, Natalie Ledwell, don Jose Ruiz, Arielle Ford, and Amit Goswami, to name a few. After three years of weekly interviews, which was like attending a deep spiritual school itself, these thought leaders and soul expanders helped to change my life in profound ways. I have integrated their wisdom and sacred gifts into my very being and am thrilled to be able to share what I have learned and how I have grown.

One thing I learned from Jacob Israel Liberman is that we are all the same height, which is an expression meaning that we all carry the same importance in this life. We are all in this together, and together we can help to change humanity as we know it. As we focus on healing ourselves, we become a clearer conduit to allow love and healing to flow through us and to help heal and raise the vibration of others as well.

Your. Healing. Matters.

There is no better time than this moment to start. Let's begin.

ONE

RISING ABOVE LIFE'S CIRCUMSTANCE

Life has knocked me down
a few times. It showed
me things I never wanted
to see. I experienced
sadness and failures.
But one thing for sure,
I always get up.

Unknown

It all happened in a tornado of emotion and fury. My brother and I had been sleeping for the greater part of the night when we heard the squeal of tires and the sounds of desperate voices from outside our bedroom windows.

"Get out of the goddamn car!" It was my father's voice, booming and panicked, that shattered our slumber. My brother came into my room, and we watched from the second story dusty window as our own fear began to unfold with the horror of the scene below. Our mother was in the car attempting to back out of the driveway with our father sprawled across the hood in an unnatural pose, trying desperately to hold on to the windshield wipers, the antenna, the cracked side view mirror.

1

With one fist he pounded on the front windshield.

"Stop this fucking car! This is not the way to deal with this! Come inside and just talk to me!" The maroon Volvo came to a screeching halt, and I watched in disbelief as my mother stumbled from the car. At first, I wondered if she had been drinking because she looked so off balance, somehow disoriented. But as she slowly walked up the driveway, I saw that her body was shaking, and her shoulders were shuddering with the sobs that racked her body.

"How could you do this to me?!" she sobbed. "Why?! Why? She was my friend," she cried, choking on the words, dripping with pain.

I looked at my brother as his eyes filled with tears. Their volume rushed the rims of his eyelids, and their immensity spilled down his face and dampened the chest of his blue and red pajamas. He was nine. Being the older sister, I stood there in the dark, strong enough for both of us. I turned from the window. No tears availed themselves to me, just a hard steel chill that began in my gut and eventually rose to my chest and took full residence in my heart. It was at that moment, my brother and I knew that our lives, the most innocent, joyful childhood we had shared, would from this point on be forever changed, and irreversibly broken.

GOLDEN BEGINNINGS

I had always felt like one of the lucky ones. I was born into an educated, upper middle-class family where there was an abundance of love, attention, and connection to go around. We were a happy family and from all outside appearances, in many ways, the model family. My parents were involved in our sports (me: basketball, softball, and soccer, and my brother: football, basketball, and baseball). We spent most weekends in the mountains, up Poudre Canyon where my father loved to fish for rainbow trout, or at our ranch on the Western Slope of Colorado.

We skied; we went to the ocean; we had family dinners together every night. I grew up with grandparents, aunts, uncles, and cousins around me constantly. My parents gave lavish parties where they hired a live musician to play in the corner of the grand room, while my brother and I hid under the dining room table and drank the ice from their leftover drinks. Such fun!

My parents attended every ballet, jazz dance, and piano recital I was in, and my mother led my 4-H cooking and crocheting classes. It seems like my young life was always on stage and always performing for them, a dynamic that followed me a great deal of my life.

But most of all, I was a daddy's girl. I adored my father. Wherever he was, I wanted to go. He was a professor at Colorado State University, and I went with him to his office any chance I could to draw on his chalk boards and keep him company while he graded papers. If he was out raking the yard, I was out helping him collect the leaves. If he was working on his workbench, I was right there beside him. Even when he shaved in the morning, I wanted to be right there with him. He would lather up his face and then mine and I would "shave" with a little plastic toothbrush case that had an edge on one side, so I felt like I was really shaving. I was his little shadow, his constant companion, and his little princess.

When my father took his afternoon naps on the living room floor on the weekends, I would snuggle up beside him, just to be close to him. I never slept. I just loved the feeling of safety and warmth I felt, like everything in the world was alright. By ten years old, I was also dad's movie buddy. We saw *Star Wars* at the big Fox Theater in town and were so blown away by it that we sat through it twice! I saw Woody Allen movies and other R-rated movies that probably weren't quite age appropriate, but I was with my dad and that was all that mattered.

And then it all changed. When that terrible night unfolded, my life became untethered. The anchor to the ship that had been the love and safety of my family was pulled up and everything seemed to toss and turn upside down in a drowning tide of emotions. My mother, who had been married to my dad for eighteen years and absolutely adored my father and our family, became emotionally unstable. Her grief was unbearable to witness. When my father moved out, it was natural for me to move out with him. There was no one closer to me in the world. But that was all to change very shortly as well.

My soon-to-be stepmother told me she considered me the "other woman" and that I was no longer number one in my father's life. From the moment we moved in with my stepmother, I was no longer allowed to talk to my father alone. I was no longer allowed to be with him alone, and to this day, there have been fewer than a handful of times that I was allowed to talk to him on the phone without her on the other line.

At sixteen, I went to stay with my mom for a couple of weeks during the summer. It was at that time that my dad and stepmom decided to move to Austin, Texas. They pulled up in the driveway of my mom's house one evening, unannounced, as I was getting ready for a date. They refused to get out of the car but honked their horn for me to come out and I did so, wrapped merely in a towel, as I had just gotten out of the shower. They told me of their plans and that I needed to decide if I wanted to move with them in three weeks or not. I had grown up in Fort Collins my whole life. I had gone to Preschool Academy with many of the same kids I was about to be a junior in high school with. The last thing I wanted to do at sixteen was leave my friends. My father, furious that I would "choose" to stay, backed angrily down the driveway, drove away, and refused to speak to me for the next year.

Imagine the impact that had on me. My father had been my whole world. His rejection left me feeling that there really must be something wrong with me, that I must truly be unlovable. I spent the next decade trying to earn love. I thought if I could wear the right clothes, look good enough, say the right things, and act a certain way, then I would be loveable. I thought that

I had to somehow earn love "out there" not realizing at the time that it was truly an inside job and that all the beauty, all the strength, and all the love I was seeking was already inside of me.

SAN FRANCISCO AWAKENINGS

A defining transitional moment happened to me when I was thirty-four years old. San Francisco was calling me. I had gone to a daylong seminar in Boulder that was about how we could become greater conduits of healing. We did some deep meditation practices, and I could feel my heart begin to shift and expand. At the end of the day when the presenter said there was a Sufi Healing School in San Francisco that would take the principles and practices we had learned that day to an even greater level, I signed up on the spot. My inner voice was very clear and concise in its message, "You need to do this!"

In August, a little over a month later, I flew from Denver to San Francisco and embarked on an experience that changed my life. Even though I had all the career, financial, and material success I could have wanted, my life felt empty in parts. My marriage was lonely, and I was desperately trying to find things outside of myself to fill the longing that I carried around with me. I had always been a happy person, despite all I had been through, but there was also something unsettled inside. I had an internal push to excel, to do the next "big" thing, yet no matter what I accomplished, I was still haunted by the feeling of never being enough.

When I arrived at the Healing School, I was greeted by Dr. Jaffe, the man that would be leading us for the week. He shook my hand as I walked into the auditorium and held on to it even after we shook... long enough that I felt a little uncomfortable. He gazed into my eyes, and it felt like he was staring straight into my soul.

When the moment finally ended, we all took our seats, and Dr. Jaffe began the introduction to our week's program. About twenty minutes in, he suddenly stopped speaking and pointed into the audience. "Hey you," he said. "You in the blue coat... I have a message for you." I looked all around me for someone who was wearing a blue coat and then slowly my gaze came to my own lap and then my blue coat. Oh crap! I was the one in the blue coat! "I am supposed to give you a message," he repeated, "and the message is..."

I couldn't hear him.

I asked the woman beside me what he had said and before she could say anything, Dr. Jaffe chuckled and said, "My dear, what I want you to know is..."

Again, I couldn't hear what he was saying. By this time, a few people were laughing, and he addressed the whole group, "This is obviously difficult for her to hear. What I am trying to say is..."

And at that moment, all of the air conditioning units in the room came on and NO ONE could hear him! Everyone burst out laughing and Dr. Jaffe invited the forty of us that were in attendance to come up to the stage and sit below him on the stairs that led up to it. When we were all seated, and everyone had settled down, he said, "The message I have for you, that you have been so resistant to hearing is this: stop trying."

Stop trying.

I had been working my ass off for so long trying to prove to everyone in the world that I was of value, worthy of love and attention, that I could not hear what it was that I most needed to do. Stop trying. For many years I had tried to earn my dad's love. In all areas of my life, I just wanted to be perfect so someone would love me. I craved what other women had so naturally with their fathers: someone that thought they hung the moon, supported them, was their cheerleader and confidant... someone to love them unconditionally.

It became an empowering moment in my life. I knew clearly in my soul that it was up to me to truly start loving myself first, from the inside out, and that would create the sense of love and fulfillment I craved. I realized I would never find it "out there," and what needed to change was my focus and my narrative which kept me tied to seeking external worth.

What has always struck me as interesting is that no matter what I have gone through, I continue to believe in the good in people and the good in life. Perhaps it was inherent within me, the little girl who always loved nature, animals, the sky, and others. Even in the hardest of times, when I couldn't see myself, I could always see the beauty in those around me. It was easy to love others and to be in deep gratitude for all that I had. I was then aware that that was only half of the equation. It was important that I had a huge loving heart for others, but that wasn't enough. It wasn't until I learned how to more deeply love myself that I truly began to heal, to truly move from surviving the pain, to fully thriving in my life.

LESSONS ALONG THE WAY

At twenty-five, I was working at The Care Unit psychiatric hospital in Aurora, Colorado, as a mental health worker on the locked-down adolescent unit. I was the only person not master's level that was a part of the mental health therapy team and I considered it a huge honor. We were a residential facility, and these were the days before managed care, so most adolescents lived with us from six to nine months until their insurance ran out.

I had one of my first lessons in fierceness when a seventeen-year-old tough kid came on to the unit my first year there. He was brought to the hospital from a rough side of Chicago where he had been a gang member. The rumor was that he had shot other people and gotten away with it. Reggie was a big, black kid, a good four inches taller than me (and I'm 5'8") and outweighed me by at least one hundred pounds. I was afraid of him. One night, the staff was helping get the kids into their rooms when I noticed Reggie was hanging out at the end of the hallway. I approached him slowly and said in an even voice,

"Reggie, you need to get in your room. It's lights out in fifteen minutes."

Reggie looked at me with dead eyes and with a loud booming voice said, "Fuck you, bitch!" I gulped. I could feel my heart pound in my ears and sweat begin to pool under my arms. He took a menacing step towards me.

"Reggie, just get in your room and get some sleep," I said firmly, although I felt anything but strong. He paused and took me in, as if to assess if I would break or not. I locked eyes with him and held my breath.

For whatever reason, he turned and went into his room. *Thank God!* I went into the staff break room and shattered into tears. I don't know what I would have done if he would have continued to oppose me. I knew this kid could probably hurt me if he chose to.

The next day, I told my friend Dawn, who was the activity therapist, what had happened with Reggie the night before. She said, "I know just what to do! During the high ropes course today, we are going to get the two of you up on the pamper pole together!"

The pamper pole consisted of two telephone poles that went up about thirty feet. At about twenty-five feet apart, each person is harnessed into safety straps and then they climb the telephone poles. Once up on top, there are two wires suspended between the two poles (one for your feet to walk on, and one to help guide your hands). The purpose of this high ropes challenge is for two people to go up on opposite sides, go out on the wire, and then when they meet in the middle, help guide each other around the other's body to the opposite side and then be belayed down to the ground. This seemed like a terrible idea! I was sure Reggie was going to kill me. Somehow, he would find out how to loosen my harness and would throw me to my death.

That day, when it came time for the ropes course activities, I showed up in my harness and began the ascent to the top of the pole, with Reggie doing the same just twenty-five feet from me. Then, something interesting happened. When Reggie got to the top of the pole, he froze, and then he began to cry. Reggie was terrified of heights. He was sure that at the top of that pole, he had just climbed to his own death, not mine. With some coercing from the staff and other adolescents below, and tears still in his eyes, Reggie started towards me on the wire. As our bodies met at the middle of the wire, I held my breath. Both of us trembled with fear for different reasons, we worked together to maneuver our bodies around each other and helped one another get to the other side.

With cheers from down below, we were both belayed down to the ground. When we were untethered from the ropes, Reggie ran over to me and swooped me up in his arms. We hugged with tear-filled eyes, happy to be alive, and somehow bonded through overcoming our fears in this shared experience.

After the ropes course, Reggie and I went back to the adolescent unit and just sat on the floor at the end of the hallway talking with one another. He was different then: vulnerable and able to access his feelings and share his own traumatic life experiences with me. I was different too. I learned that when we show up and face our fears, no matter how big they may seem, in the end, they can guide us to a whole new awareness of an inner strength we didn't even know we possessed. Going through the fear and doing it anyway may just lead us to miracles.

LISTENING TO INTUITION

There were many lessons I learned from my time working at The Care Unit. One of the biggest happened when I decided to leave.

My aunt owned a condo in Vail, Colorado. It was actually more than a condo, it was a three-level twin home that slept fourteen people in its six bedrooms, very comfortably. For fifteen years it was a beautiful part of my life, and that of my family and friends. Something that, as a twenty-five-year-old single mom living on $50 a week after all my bills were paid, I could never have afforded.

I will never forget that weekend. Thirteen of my friends, some I had known from high school or college, and some of my dear friends from Denver, all happily filled this home. We had an amazing weekend of skiing, ice skating, making amazing dinners, and drinking margaritas at the top of the mountain. Laughter filled the air of the vaulted ceilings and a warm fire blazed in the big moss rock fireplace every night. It was all perfect.

Until it wasn't.

The third and last night we were there, as I got ready to go to bed, I began to cry. My friend Elle, who I was sharing the room with, asked with tenderness, "What is going on? What is bringing this on?" I told her I had no idea but that something very strong inside of me was telling me I needed to leave Denver and move back to Fort Collins. "Why in the world would you want to do that?!" She inquired. "You have an amazing job, amazing friends! You are the only non-master's leveled person on the therapy staff. What would make you want to leave?!" While all of that was true and wonderful, something deep inside of me was sounding the call, loudly. I needed to leave Denver. Period.

The next morning when I woke up, I called my mother who still lived in Fort Collins. "Mom, I don't know why, but I have had the strongest message that I need to leave Denver and move home." It was January 14 and the lease at my apartment was ending February 1. I could go back to work on the fifteenth and give them my two weeks' notice and move back to Fort Collins.

The voice, still loud in my head, was saying my time in Denver was done and it was essential I get back home as soon as possible. I held my breath and waited for her to speak.

"Actually, our renter's lease is up February 1," she said. "He just gave us notice yesterday that he will be moving out and not renewing it. You can just move in there."

And that is exactly what I did. I followed this deep intuition and guidance that was beyond me, and I left my job, my Denver friends, and my old apartment and moved my four-year-old daughter and me back home. Exactly three weeks later, the adolescent unit was shut down, never to reopen, and all of the wonderful girlfriends I had made there were laid off and forced to find other jobs. The front page of the *Rocky Mountain News* read, "Psychiatric Abuses Charged." The adolescent unit's higher ups had been using scouts to find kids all over the nation that needed psychiatric care and were bringing them to The Care Unit. Then the children would stay on the unit until all of their insurance had run out. Those scouts were being paid $5,000 per kid to bring them in. None of it ethical or legal.

Here's the thing. If I would have stayed, I would have signed a new lease and would not have been able to afford the rent. I would have been panicking to find another job to support my daughter and I. I would have been in survival mode, and it would have been traumatic. Instead, I was settled in my new home in Fort Collins, had found a job the first week I was there, and was thriving.

Lesson learned.

Even when others didn't understand my decision, I became fierce in my knowingness, that when that voice spoke to me in a clear direction, I listened to it. I began to trust my intuition and my higher GPS to lead the way and guide me on the next steps of my journey. Guidance from my higher self has led to the most amazing experiences of my life and has shown up every time I needed it—even times I didn't know I needed it. It has helped guide me through the greatest storms of my life and has gotten me through to the other side.

We all have this inner GPS available to us. It's that small voice that whispers to us when we are still and if we don't listen, it will speak a little louder, and if we continue to ignore it, it finally comes as a brick to the head.

Let's listen.

BEYOND LIFE LESSONS

One of the biggest lessons I have learned came from my daughter Acacia, when she was four years old. Shortly after we moved back to Fort Collins, I received the horrible news that my Aunt Gwen, only forty-six at the time, had been diagnosed with terminal cancer. I had been talking to my mother while I was in the bathtub on one of those huge old portable phones. As I hung up, Acacia came into the bathroom and sat on the tub.

I didn't have time to wipe my tears. She took me in with her big blue eyes and her face softened and her voice took on a tone I had never heard before.

"Why are you crying mommy?"

She had never seen me cry before. We stared into each other's eyes. I had always spoken to her as authentically as I could.

"Oh, honey. Mommy just never wants anyone to die," I said. I had never spoken to her about death, and it was not something that had come into our lives before. She sat there still and solidly, looking at me with disbelief.

"But mommy, we never die."

My heart skipped a beat. I looked at her and saw the strangest look cross her face, a knowingness I had never seen before.

Even though we had never gone to church together or talked about God or an afterlife, I said, "I know sweetheart. We go to heaven." Acacia just looked at me like I had no idea what I was talking about.

"Mom. There is no heaven. When I was with God, I was a light up in the sky." I felt myself suck in my breath. Then she said something that changed my life forever.

"Do you remember your other mother, Dorthey?"

Dorthey had been my grandmother who had died when I was thirteen. Acacia had never known her or even known *of* her. My grandfather had remarried a woman named Lucille the year after her death, and the only great grandma Acacia knew was Grandma Cille. Her phrase stunned me. *Your other mother, Dorthey.*

She continued innocently, "Well, her light was in the sky with me. So God took some of her light and put it with my light and then I got to come down and be your daughter."

What was happening? There was no way she could have known any of this. It was as if time had stopped, and this little voice was speaking from a greater realm than I had ever experienced.

I couldn't speak.

I burst out crying again and hugged her, told her everything was okay, and then called my mother back. Dorthey was her mother. Astonished, we both cried together at this miracle spoken from the mouth of babes.

Interesting to note: *Acacia* is the Greek word for immortality. It is the tree of life in Africa. My little four-year-old was teaching me about the immortality of our souls which created a huge shift in my awareness and in my ability to live fiercely. In that moment, I lost my fear of death. Now, of course, I don't want to die; I am thoroughly enjoying this life, but something changed in me that allowed me to live life from a more expanded perspective. From that point on, I have been able to live fully in the present moment, because I am no longer afraid of what the future might bring.

At forty-five I hiked to the top of Longs Peak, I scuba dive, white water river raft, have traveled the world, and last year, on my fifty-third birthday, I did a front flip on the trampoline for the first time in over thirty years! It was awesome! By no means am I reckless with this knowledge I gained from Acacia, nor do I encourage anyone to take any unnecessary risks or do anything they are truly uncomfortable with. But I do live full out and I encourage others to do the same. I speak professionally on stage, write books, record radio shows, make films, and meet the people who have been my role models because I am fierce about living this life I was given! I am not afraid to take risks or explore new places, things, or people. I jump into life each day with an open heart and with both feet forward. Being unafraid of death has allowed me to plug into life more fully. With reverence, and respect for this precious world we live in, I savor each moment.

THE GIFT

What continues to amaze me is that these incredibly difficult pain points in our lives—once healed—become the gifts that we give back to the world. It's through these challenges that we can glean wisdom and help other people heal and gain perspective in their own lives. It's often at times in our darkest moments—when we feel vulnerable and afraid—that our breakthroughs happen.

We don't have to be afraid during these times. If we can step back from the resistance that says, "I don't want to feel this way! I don't want this to be my life!" and pause long enough to ask ourselves instead, "How do I best get through these twenty-four hours?" or even, "How do I best get through this moment… this breath?" We may then begin to befriend the present moment which aids in the healing of our lives because we are not resisting what is. It quickens the healing process when we embrace whatever has shown up. As we open to the pain, we can transmute and glean the gifts waiting on the other side. When we find the gifts in our ongoing story and see our journey as an eclectic gathering of wisdom, we truly become fiercer and more empowered in our lives.

As a therapist and transformational life coach, I have heard people say, "Well, you have it all together. This is easy for you!" The truth is, we never arrive at "all together." It is so important to know that there are continued lessons. As long as we are breathing, we have something to learn. Healing happens in layers; therefore, we never quite get to the point where it is all figured out. There are times we are in a wonderful place in our lives, and then something surfaces that needs to be healed. I love how my partner always says, "What a blessing!" when I share a trigger with him. He reminds me that the trigger is a new opening that has revealed an opportunity that I can shine the light of awareness and compassion on and heal.

Let's give ourselves permission to be imperfect and to *not* have everything figured out. Let's acknowledge that life is messy, and let's create a space where we can be fragile and more vulnerable with one another. From these places, we are able to give each other the gift of authenticity, transparency, and a deeper connection to this human experience we all share. Live this amazing and beautiful life. Embrace the complete experience. Breathe into and through the difficult times. Feel them fully and then release them. Learn from those moments. Savor the joy and know that love is what makes it all worthwhile.

This is our time on this earth, and we are the co-creators in everything we experience. When we embrace the fullness of this life—the painful and the passionate, the ecstasy and the angst—we allow our spirits to actualize their true purpose. This life is often experienced in duality. What if we just loved the entire experience of it? What if by embracing whatever showed up in our lives, we were able to live in a flow state with more joy and serenity?

There is ecstatic joy when we play full-out and allow ourselves to enjoy all the richness that is available in this life. How would life be different, lived fully in the moment, without fear holding us back? What would it feel like to live this fierce and fantastic life without limits?

My life has been full of challenges and heartache, and it has also been full of tons of love and moments of tremendous joy. Remember the Unsinkable Molly Brown from *The Titanic* who lived through the horrendous sinking of that ship and went on to thrive in her life? We can all become the Unsinkable Molly Browns in our own lives. We can become aware that life will be full of beauty and pain, difficulties and divine moments, and that the polarities are just a part of being fully alive. Like Molly, we can be open to the awareness that we can make it through anything and that we have the absolute ability to keep creating our best lives. We can go beyond surviving the icebergs in our lives, and fully thrive in this day, in this moment, and create something beautiful.

Take a Moment

What are your guideposts?

We have all experienced meaningful moments that have brought us clarity, insight, or that became a pivotal point of knowingness along our journey. To bring greater awareness of the moments that have brought you wisdom, guidance, and transformation, I invite you to try this journaling exercise.

Make a list of significant guideposts along your life path. What moments made a difference in your life, or led you to make an important decision that helped change your life? See how the dots connect to lead you right to where you are in the present moment. Sometimes we are unaware of the miracles that have unfolded in our lives. Start at the beginning of your life and allow yourself to discover those moments that truly made a difference.

As we see this divine path unfold in our lives, we realize, we have never been truly alone and that whether the events were challenging and painful, or joyful and amazing, they have all held meaning and valuable lessons that have helped create who we are today.

EXPANDING OUR SENSE OF SELF

You can also expand this exercise by listing the times you have shown up for yourself, times you were strong, courageous, or fierce, or times you contributed to and made a difference in the life of someone else. Look back and take an inventory of all the things you can think of that helped ignite the sparks in you.

These could be moments when you found your voice and spoke up, or you put yourself through school, or accomplished something against all odds. Let yourself float back to the times in your life when you made the decision to keep going, overcame a difficulty, or fought for someone or something you loved.

We are all fierce. We all have this fierce nature inside of us. Sometimes we forget that despite how much we may have covered it up, our fierce self has shown through in moments and refused to be silenced. In each of our lives, even if only for a moment, the beautiful spark that is the essence of each one of us, has caught flame and we have lived fully lit up.

TWO

YOU WERE BORN FIERCE. WHAT HAPPENED?

You were not born to please,
You were brought here to
Disrupt, awaken, and speak truth,
And so when you are asked to quiet down,
I hope you grow louder.
You are an entire symphony that needs no applause.

Aiji Mayrock

Most of us can remember a time before we entered elementary school where we didn't feel the social pressure to be anything other than who we were. If we wanted to sing, dance, or roll on the rug, there was a certain permission that youth afforded us, and we flowed through our days just being who we were without reservation. We were alive with wonder, and we were fearless as we explored and adventured out into the world. We wanted to touch, taste, smell, and experience everything in this playground we call life. We made friends easily with kids, kittens, and daddy-long-legs. We radiated our beautiful essence to the world.

Inevitably, as we grow up, we are put into social situations, school, church, family gatherings, or experiences where that sense of just being who we are comes into question. Somewhere along the way, we start getting information about how we look, feel, act, or how we show up in the world, that is deemed by others as, "not good enough." This "not good enough" is often carried throughout our entire lives (although often subconsciously) and begins to become our narrative of how we see ourselves in the world.

So, what happens to us? Where does this beautiful wild and fierce nature go?

I remember being a little girl at my grandparents' house in Nebraska. The very clear message at the dinner table was, "Children are to be seen and not heard." The expectation was that we were supposed to sit (sometimes for up to two hours) while the adults chatted at dinner, and only when they were done, were we allowed to leave the table to go play. This could be excruciating! At six, with a three-year-old brother, this task to sit still seemed impossible! But our grandparents' disapproving looks, and scolding words were enough to keep us quiet and barely moving.

After swallowing her own voice around this for years, it wasn't until my mother became fierce herself, and finally stood up to my grandparents that this dynamic changed. "When my children are done eating, I am going to let them go play. It doesn't make sense to keep them here!" Such an empowering experience for my mother, but the damage to our little souls had already been done. The message was already encoded in my brother and I that in order to be loved and approved of, we had to keep quiet.

Other big messages in my life came when I was seven and my family moved to Corvallis, Oregon. I was a confident, happy-go-lucky little girl, in love with all my friends, my animals, and my family, but most importantly, I was in love with myself. Before the move, I loved to dress up, play make-believe, be silly, laugh out loud, and sing at the top of my lungs. I thought

I was beautiful and thought everyone else was beautiful too.

The first day of school as I walked with my little brother down the wooded path to the Montessori school, I was stopped by a girl my age who said to me, "You have a long nose, and you are wearing your socks all wrong! You are supposed to roll them down, not have them to your knees!" Interestingly, she didn't say either of these statements with malice, just a matter of fact that some things about me were not quite right.

I remember feeling confused and embarrassed that there was something wrong with how I dressed and how I looked. I had always worn my socks with my dresses that way, but suddenly, it wasn't okay. The confident little girl I had arrived as in Corvallis, was changed a bit that day. For the first time in my life, I looked at myself in a critical way and wished I was different. I began to shut down a little bit of the light that was the essence of me. I became aware for the first time that "I wasn't good enough." And so, it began—with a single erosive sentence—to shape my self-concept.

We are in theta brainwave state for the first seven years of our lives. This is a time when we are totally susceptible and vulnerable to input from those around us, and we believe their feedback and criticism of us as the "truth." This is where the shutdown of our true fierce nature can begin. We want to fit in. We want to belong. We begin to receive the messages from outside of us as to how we "should" act, feel, and look, and we begin to adapt. This pressure to give up ourselves in order to fit in can happen at a young age. We may not realize we have lost a part of ourselves and our essential shine until decades later when we feel like we have imposter syndrome and are living someone else's life because we have lost perspective of being ourselves in the world. We have lost that fierce little spark, the part of us that wasn't afraid to laugh and play and run full out.

I'm reminded of my daughter Hailey at four years old, standing on top of the picnic bench, shouting for everyone to, "Listen!" and then singing, "Take Me Out to the Ball Game" at the top of her lungs. Even though she only knew half the words and thought the song went, "Take me out to the ball game, take me out to the garage!" it was awesome! Those were *her* words, and she sang them with full abandon to anyone who would listen.

We can think about what "not good enough" messages we received as children and notice what messages may still be present. Caretakers, family, friends, teachers, and coaches— even with great intentions—can leave us with the message that we weren't smart enough, fast enough, attractive enough, or driven enough. For us to change our limiting beliefs, we first need to excavate our subconscious a bit to become aware of what these negative thoughts are that are driving us in our self-doubt or self-deprecation so we can become conscious of how we want to change them. How we can start rescripting those narratives, start redefining and rewriting our own messages of worthiness is what this chapter is about.

BELONGINGNESS

We all have an inherent need to belong. Our very survival throughout millennia often depended on our ability to stay with the group, our community, or in a tribe that could protect us. In Maslow's hierarchy of needs, belongingness is one of the most important things motivating human behavior. By belonging to a group, we feel we are a part of something bigger and more important than ourselves. So, what starts to happen if we feel like we don't really belong or fit in? We change. We give parts of ourselves away. We compromise what is important to us so we can win others' approval. It is part of our survival instinct.

It is important to watch the swing of the pendulum over to the other side which can become the narrative of "I don't need anyone else!" and the buy-in to rugged individualism as a way that we can define ourselves. In our society there are strong messages (especially for men) that say, "In order to be successful in the world, you need to be totally self-sufficient and independent." To depend on someone else gets confused with being co-dependent, which couldn't be further from the truth. The true definition of co-dependence is characterized by excessive emotional or psychological reliance on a partner, typically one who requires support because of illness or addiction.

We are all *interdependent*. We need one another. Science has proven that all biological systems are interdependent. Plants, animals, and humans depend on one another to survive. A sense of belonging is one of our greatest human needs, just like food, water, and shelter. It is an important part of our very survival. So, know that the deep urge to fit in comes from a very hardwired part of our DNA, it is a natural and normal instinct to who we are as a species.

In 2020, the highest rate of suicide per capita was in Alaska, followed by South Dakota, Montana, and Wyoming. These are states where there is a sparse population and the concept of "Pull yourself up by your bootstraps" as a way to deal with emotions when things get hard. But at what cost? When we isolate ourselves, or don't reach out when struggling, we can fall into depression and despair. There are countless studies on what happens to newborn babies who are deprived of touch and have failure to thrive. I believe without one another and a sense of belonging, we will have failure to thrive as well. When we feel we belong (to a family, a group, or a community) it gives us a deeper sense of security and helps us cope with the intense challenges and hardships we face, because we are not facing them alone.

So how does being fierce interface with belongingness and what does that look like? It is an act of inner strength to admit when we are hurting or feeling lonely and need help. It takes guts to do a fearless internal inventory to look at the places where we have messed up or need to make amends with someone to heal a relationship. This work is not for sissies. It takes courage to continue to show up and be transparent, real, raw, and to express our thoughts, feelings, and needs. It takes strength to reach out to others and *allow* them to help and admit when we are unable to solve a problem or deal with a situation.

When we become fierce, we face the things that scare us, we lean into the places we feel weak instead of avoiding them. We do hard things that feel uncomfortable, like asking for help. And when faced with the feelings of fear in finding our voice and speaking our truth we DO IT ANYWAY and move through the fear to freedom. When we hold onto ourselves, when we show up and become our own self-advocates, when we listen to that still, inner voice that guides us, we become a powerful force in the world and in our own lives.

THE LOLLIPOP THEORY

Years ago, I made up what I call The Lollipop Theory. It has to do with how we compromise ourselves or give up parts of ourselves just to fit in. When we are little kids, we *LOVE* lollipops! We don't care who sees one hanging out of our mouths. We can sit there with a big slobbery grin on our faces because nothing else matters. We just love lollipops. Then as we get a little older, into junior high or high school, or even college, we are like, "No way am I having a lollipop! Lollipops are for babies, and I am just too cool for lollipops." Eventually, we mature enough that we are able to say, "I can have a lollipop if I want one." We can decide for ourselves if we want to have a lollipop, or we don't.

The choice is ours. The same is true for other behaviors and actions. We can still play as adults. We can laugh out loud, sing, dance, and be spontaneous. We know when we need to be more serious when the situation calls for it. That is the beautiful thing. We have a choice. We can have the best of both worlds. Being a fully embodied adult means we can let ourselves play full-out when the time is right and when we need to step into a more serious version of ourselves we can easily do that as well.

WHEN WE COME BACK TO OURSELVES

Pedram Shojai, also known as The Urban Monk, expressed

in an interview with me the extreme pressure he felt from his parents to become a doctor, lawyer, or engineer because as an immigrant, the expectations were extremely high for what they considered success. He said he felt he needed to be a doctor because his parents had sacrificed so much to bring the family to America. As he was doing his internship, he noticed his supervising doctor was a miserable human being with a lot of narcissism and ego that went around "jacking people up on morphine." Pedram shared that that experience broke him. Looking at that doctor, he realized he never wanted to be like this man, and this made him stop and question why he had been working so hard at something that wasn't his passion.

Even though he didn't come from a religious background, it made him ask questions about God. He said he asked God, "Yo' man, if you are there, I could sure use a clue. I could sure use some help!" and that was when a book fell out of a bookshelf at a bookstore and changed his life. That moment and that book began a trail of breadcrumbs which led him on a whole new path and his life began to unfold in a beautiful new direction. He traveled to ashrams in India, studied with Buddhist and Hindu masters, and later became a Taoist monk. Oftentimes, we think we can find happiness if we do what we are "supposed" to do and what others think is best for us and our future. Pedram's essential message was, "If you think that your happiness lies outside of you... come back." Come back to your own inner knowing and listen to the still soft voice that guides you to your own best destiny!

We can't find the fix for well-being and happiness somewhere else. We can't do things or try to figure out how to be true to ourselves and our own divine spirit and deepest essence outside of ourselves. When we tap in, slow down, find some stillness, and listen to that deeper inner voice, we can find all the direction and validation we need. We can tap into our own wild natures that will lead us on a divine path that no one else can set for us. We can learn to listen to our own souls.

Come back!

TAKE A MOMENT

It is part of human nature. We do things to fit in or to belong. We hide parts of ourselves away for fear of how others may receive (and reject) us. We give up some of the things we love or the things that bring us pleasure to avoid looking "uncool."

Where are the places in your life that you give parts of yourself up to fit in? Where do you lose your voice and swallow it down to avoid rocking the boat or having someone dislike you? Look at places where you may have "given up your lollipop." What do you want to reclaim? Notice the parts of you that used to be more spontaneous or playful. Start practicing those things that feel truer or more in alignment to your authentic self. If you always felt connected to nature as a child, spend time outdoors. Taking a walk on a trail or in your backyard and looking up at the sky and the clouds can reconnect you to that inner nature that feeds you.

Sometimes, to get in touch with what we really want to do, be, and have in our lives, we must look at what is limiting us from getting there. The following exercise is a powerful way of excavating those (sometimes subconscious) limiting beliefs and beginning to transform them.

It is often helpful to spend a few moments in meditation, perhaps remembering the messages you received as a child that helped to wire these limiting beliefs within. If you had a role model that told you as a child, "Money is the root of all evil," you may have developed an unhealthy relationship to money. Or, if your message around work was, "You have to grind to be successful," then when things came easy to you in your career, you may have rejected them or may not have seen them as truly valuable because of the old belief system. Awareness is the first key to transforming your life! Start with the awareness of what you have believed and then we will start moving towards what you would like to believe instead.

Look for beliefs that have *always* or *never* in them. The phrases "I never can get ahead," or "I'm always struggling to meet people," have in them a self-fulfilling prophecy. They are self-defeating because there is no way out. Your subconscious hears these beliefs as "the law."

Write down your limiting beliefs in the following areas:

1. Relationship

2. Career

3. Money and Finances

4. Health and Fitness

5. Spirituality

6. Self-Concept

7. Family

After you write down your limiting beliefs, think of what you would like to believe about yourself in those areas instead and write those down in positive, present-tense language (as if all your new beliefs were true now). It helps to write this out in a narrative style, as if it were a year into the future and you were telling someone how grateful and thankful you were for your incredible new life.

For example, saying and thinking phrases such as "I am so grateful that I live in abundance. I am thankful for my healthy relationship with money," or "I continue to attract wonderful people into my life," will begin to carve new neural pathways that affirm your new beliefs, and you will begin to see evidence of these beliefs in your external world as you practice them. Reading statements like these out loud daily and allowing yourself to marinate on the good feelings will help to anchor this new belief system into your being. First thing in the morning, and last thing before you go to sleep, your brain is going into Theta brainwave state where it is more susceptible to input. These are the best times to recite your affirmations. Putting them to music (without lyrics) is even more powerful. Our mind can be a slippery slope and dismiss the positive affirmations that it doesn't yet believe. When you play music, this critical voice seems to be drowned out and the affirmations will "stick" even better.

Research tells us that it takes twenty-one to thirty days for something to become a habit. That is why most diets or exercise programs are that length. Your mind will begin to integrate this information and then it will be automated into a new belief system. Notice the breadcrumbs of positivity that show up in your life and lead you to a greater expansion of your true self and your true nature, which is more lit up, and more fully expressing the amazing essence that is YOU!

We all have our story. It is woven inextricably to us and can become the very fiber of our being. Sometimes we identify so strongly with our story that we are not able to see the "truth" of who we are which is far beyond "our story."

You can begin right now to start a new narrative.

When we stop and take inventory of our own lives, a strange alchemy begins to take place. When we rewrite our negative beliefs and old scripts, we begin to excavate that true self and wild nature we were born with. We build inner resilience and grit, we become more expansive and we find our sense of belonging, even at first, if only to ourselves, and experience a sense of deeper authenticity. When we are able to listen to our inner GPS, it can lead us to fulfilling our purpose and living a life fully lit up. When we do this, we ignite our passion and we become a fierce soul, living fully in this world.

THREE

OUR RELATIONSHIP WITH POWER

There are powers inside of you which, if you could discover and use,
would make of you everything you ever dreamed or imagined you could
become.

Orison Swett Marden

It has been the focus of therapists, healers, and spiritual leaders to help us move out of our heads and into our hearts. We talk about the heart acting as the individual's center for compassion, empathy, love, and forgiveness. We need more of that in our world. We need to cultivate more of that within ourselves. I truly believe that love is the answer.

But what if love isn't enough? What if healing our heart is only the first step towards making substantial changes within ourselves and for our planet? How do we become clearer conduits for love and healing to flow through us and out into the world?

Love is easy in some respects. Love feels like a warm puppy snuggled in your lap or a fluffy blanket wrapped around you as you sit by a fire on a rainy day. Power is more difficult to describe, and our relationship with power, even trickier. The power I am speaking about is not "having power OVER someone," it is about accessing your own personal power by accessing and living through your heart. It is the ability to live your purpose, and the power to listen to your own heart as you create and express who you truly are. It is the power to live through love.

POWER CONFUSED

One of the biggest issues with claiming power, owning it, and living it through love is that many people, because of early childhood traumas, have a distorted view of what *power* actually means. They may even have a visceral reaction to the word, or they may avoid positions or people who represent it. For example, an adult who was sexually abused as a child, may have a very different experience of power if their trauma has not been healed.

As children, when someone has power over us that is abusive, we may avoid feelings of power as adults because it is confused with a feeling of abusive domination over others, and it becomes something to be avoided rather than embraced. Power in this way is seen as destructive energy and something that leaves victims in its wake, not something that can be a force of good within us and our world.

Abused children can become adults who are afraid to be in their own power because they correlate it to *being* an abuser. Power becomes something that has negative consequences and is not seen as a positive power within. It becomes a power to manipulate, control, and abuse others.

It is important that we understand our programming around power. What messages did we receive around power as a child? In my own experience growing up, there were strong messages around, "Be smart, but not too smart." "Stand out, but don't try to be the center of attention." "Speak up but laugh and talk quietly." Those were confusing and conflicting messages about what it meant to be in my power.

I also heard the message throughout my childhood that I was too sensitive. So, in order to feel more powerful, I had to cut off from my heart and protect it with a false sense of power. It felt like power because it became a strong fortress of protection, but it was truly only a false front, that in the end, cut me off from having greater and deeper experiences of love.

We often see power portrayed in the media by someone being very narcissistic and not caring about others. Political and military power can be viewed in this negative way as well with the power of a few controlling the many and leaving many feeling helpless, hopeless, and very unempowered. Considering what has been happening in our world, many people are afraid to share their opinions of power on social media or even with friends and family for fear of being ostracized and shut down.

We give away our power when we let others dictate how we feel about ourselves through their words and actions, and when we lose our voice or become small so others won't be threatened by us. When we play small, we are depriving others of our gifts that could truly serve them and ourselves. The world needs each one of us to show up in our power and to share the greatest version of ourselves with one another.

So how *do* we find and heal our relationship with power? How do we become a powerful force of healing within ourselves and in the world?

ACCESSING OUR POWER CENTER

It can be very difficult to heal our relationship with power because so often we experience power through our intellect or our ego. An essential part of accessing true power is to move from our heads down into our hearts. This process was evident during a session with a client of mine when I led him through a three-year visualization. The moment he looked at his present self through his future self's eyes, he instantly broke down in tears.

"Tell me what's happening," I inquired.

"When I turned around and saw myself in the present moment," he responded, "I saw how constricted I was. How I kept everything at a cerebral level and had truly shut down my heart to protect it."

It was a cathartic moment watching him allow the walls he had built around his heart to come crashing down. His desire to open his heart and feel what he had been shut down to was so strong, and the awareness of the incredible prison those walls had created was immense. It was an opening into a new and expanded life for him and a deep pathway to profound healing. It was a portal that enabled him to access his personal power. As he began to live more through his heart and was able to be vulnerable enough to feel his feelings, he experienced more love, more connection with his wife and colleagues, and he decided to follow his passion for world-wide consulting instead of staying with his teaching job and went on to experience a life that was far more fulfilling than he had ever experienced.

This work of living from and through our hearts becomes the first step toward accessing our personal power. Power does not come from the ego, although it may feel like it. The ego can also be very fragile and shatter if challenged by opposing forces. When we step into our humility, and we surrender to the present moment (a concept we will explore more thoroughly in later chapters), it becomes an entry point to our personal power.

If we are stressing and worrying about the future, we are not in our power. If we are ruminating about the past, we are also not in our power. It is only through acceptance and surrender to the present moment, that we become free to problem solve, to choose our path, and to design a new way forward.

As we release our external programming of happiness, and to things we thought would make us more powerful, we begin to truly experience a sense of inner power, and we deeply realize that creating happiness is an inside job. Powerful indeed.

UNDERSTANDING THE POWER WITHIN US

We were born with power and energy that is always available to us. In many cultures, the "energy centers" are known as *chakras* or spinning wheels of energy and are located along the spine representing the coming together of the physical and spiritual. When our chakras are open and in balance, we are healthy and centered, life is good, and it flows easily. When our chakras are blocked or out of balance, we feel stressed, out of harmony, and out of alignment with ourselves.

Eastern culture recognizes seven chakras starting with the first (root) and extending to the seventh (crown). Each chakra has its own attributes and corresponds to systems in the body; in addition, each chakra also has a spiritual meaning or connection. The third chakra, our solar plexus, is the chakra that is considered the source of personal power. It holds within it the power of transformation, warrior energy, and strengthened self-esteem. As we focus on this chakra, we can move into a heart- and power-coherent state where love and power flow together like an infinity sign, one informing and influencing the other.

Friction-breathe into this energy center and feel the energy begin to emanate from this area. Friction breathing is sometimes called the ocean breath or *ujjayi* breath in yoga practice. Inhalation and exhalation are both done through the nose and are equal in duration, and the mouth is closed. The throat is slightly constricted as if fogging up a mirror, and the sound of the breath will begin to mimic ocean waves.

This is our life force energy and is always available to us. As we sit in silence and focus on each one of our chakras, we can feel the inner power of that chakra radiate through us and we become more aligned with our higher selves and our deepest nature. This continued practice is a gateway to feeling truly empowered. It is as close as our breath. It is the energy that is our very essence.

PRESENT MOMENT POWER

How do we access our inner power in a positive way? How can we become fiercely powerful in our passion, our love, and our expression?

We need to bring ourselves into the present moment. So often this is my conversation with my clients, "The thing you are worrying about is not happening now, but you are anxiously anticipating the worst and so if the worst happens, you won't have much emotional energy left to deal with it. If you bring yourself to the present, where most things are okay in this moment, you can relax and rejuvenate, so if the worst really does happen, you will have a reservoir inside of you in which to deal with whatever comes."

We cannot be fierce if we are worrying about the future or ruminating about the past. When we are preoccupied with thought, we are no longer in the present and that actually weakens our immune system, floods our body with cortisol and adrenaline, and wreaks havoc on our emotions. When we are present-moment focused and open to new insights and information, we are coming from a place of strength. We make better decisions about our future from a more relaxed and spacious place.

It is powerful to hold the present moment in our awareness *exactly* as it is, with no desire to change it. We can notice where our emotions show up in our bodies and instead of trying to change anything, we can just breathe into them and notice if there are other feelings or emotions underneath. Just staying with the body and the breath, actually helps release what is there. As we surrender these feelings to the present moment and let them go, we can notice we begin to find a sense of calm and from this place, a subtle joy may start to arise.

It is interesting that what brings us so much fear of the unknown is our feeling of a lack of control, when the truth is, we really don't have much control over anything outside of ourselves. "Control" in so many ways is just a myth that is soothing to us when the unknown can trigger our insecurities, anxiety, and fear.

Can we control what is happening to us tomorrow? Will we

be able to control the environment, other people's behavior? We may be able to "predict" what is happening in our schedule tomorrow, but we will not be able to control the actual events of the day. We will have to experience them moment by moment by moment.

My clients have found it amazingly helpful to practice focusing on the next twenty-four hours at hand and have found when they are able to let go of the past or future, life becomes more manageable and less overwhelming. Let's practice that right now by feeling into the belly and taking a deep breath and slowly letting it go. Take another as if taking a breath all the way down to the kneecaps and then one more down to the tips of the toes and slowly let these breaths go and see what comes up. Feeling and breathing into the here and now, promotes relaxation.

It is amazingly freeing to let go of the false sense of control and come back to what we do have power over which is our ability to choose what we focus on and to influence our state of being. By accepting the present moment as it is, we are infused with a power far beyond what we had been trying to anxiously predict and control our futures with; we are equipping ourselves with our own internal compass and this will surely help us navigate whatever rapids are ahead in our river of life.

TAKE A MOMENT

One way to bring focus and a sense of personal power into your day is a morning journaling exercise called The Three C's. It is a great way of priming your mind and allowing yourself to truly access what you need to cultivate each day and puts your well-being as a priority. Each C is a question you ask yourself.

1. How can I take CARE of myself today?

   Think about what you need to do to truly take care of you today. It may include nutritional food, exercise, meditation, time in nature, stretching, time for reflection, or anything else that nurtures your mind, body, and soul.

2. How can I CONNECT today?

   Even during the time of the pandemic, when we were unable to see each other face to face, connection was imperative for our well-being. Many times, texting isn't enough. Try to call, or use video calls for those you truly desire to connect with. There are endless studies on the importance of our social connections. We need one another!

3. How can I be CREATIVE today?

   You don't have to be an artist or a musician to be creative. I encourage you to make a playlist of ten of the songs that make you feel joy, love, or connection to your higher self.

   My partner and I have been guilty of breaking out in spontaneous dance parties in the kitchen while listening to one of these lists. Even if one of us is just chopping vegetables while the other one is cooking, we both experience flow and happiness in those moments.

You can literally be creative in the way you choose to walk your dog by choosing another path or driving a different route to work. These are all great ways to get your creative mind to engage. You can sing, dance, create art, write, or craft, or anything else that helps put you in flow. Consider establishing a morning routine of creativity. Having a morning routine helps to set up a pillar of power in your life that you can depend on. When you start the day off having yourself in your own corner, you will be unstoppable.

With all three of these, it is best to write down your answers. It's like an accountability strategy to schedule things into your day. This will help to strengthen your sense of power in the present moment and further cultivate your relationship with yourself. Its calming ability for your mind and soul are palpable and you will begin to notice the results immediately.

Healing your relationship with power can empower you to do tremendous things in your life. Remembering that all the strength, all the wisdom, and all the happiness you are seeking are already right there inside of you, will become a fierce inner strength that will allow you to be more solid in who you are. You can increase your personal power by befriending the present moment, feeling what arises within you, and focusing on accepting this moment as it is, no matter what arises. Breathe into the power center of your solar plexus, feel your own grounding to the earth. When you are defined by your inner self and not looking to the outside world to tell you who you are, or how you should feel, you become amazingly powerful indeed. The point of power is always in the present moment. You have the power to choose what you focus on. We can move out of our heads and into our hearts. Let that love flow through you, as you, and see what a fierce difference it can make in your life and in your world.

FOUR

LOVING FIERCELY

Living on purpose requires us to love fiercely,
give it all we've got and then
pass it on, as if it were a
torch, to those who follow.

Dawna Markova

When we love fiercely, we love with our full hearts. We take risks. We are an open channel to love both in and out. We invest, we believe in, and we support one another fully. We love with a passion that does not consume us, but rather ignites us in a way that it becomes a guiding force and light in our lives. To truly love fiercely, we learn that we must fall in love with our own beautiful lives and spirits and only then, can we fully embody the fierceness in which we love one another.

My first experience of this kind of fierce love was as a mother. At twenty-one years old, I had my first child. Deeply etched in the cells of my memory is the experience of having my midwife ask me to put my hands under her little arms as she was being born and deliver her from my body, out into this world. Nothing in my entire life up until that moment, could have prepared me for the fierce love I felt for my daughter instantly. When she was six weeks old, I remember thinking that nothing else in the world mattered besides taking care of her and loving her with everything inside of me. My heart was fully broken open and fully aflame.

What makes it so difficult to love this way? We may think, *Well, yeah, it's easy with your own child but try a spouse that is driving you crazy or has hurt you in some way. How do you love fiercely then?* Part of this healing begins when we realize that our hearts, like our essence, ALWAYS have the capacity to love fiercely. It is inherent in us, and it is our true essence.

LOVING LONGITUDINALLY

Imagine the feeling of losing a loved one, not to death, but to banishment because of an incident that happened decades earlier that was handled improperly. That is exactly what my friend Silvia experienced when her beloved husband of twelve years, best friend, and father of her children was deported back to El Salvador eight years ago and still has not been allowed to reenter the USA.

Silvia met her husband in 1998 and they enjoyed a rich, solid, and loving relationship and eventually married. They planned their life together, bought a house, started businesses, and brought a beautiful daughter into the world. In 2013, Silvia's husband, after forty years of working in the U.S. and paying taxes, was deported back to El Salvador, where he was born. It was also the place, where at eight years old, a group of men had burst into his family's home during dinner and murdered his father right in front of him. After this horrific trauma, he was sent to the United States to live with an uncle in Los Angeles.

The main reason he was deported was because at eighteen, he had been in the wrong place at the wrong time. He was playing handball in a park when the police did a sweep of the park and found one of the other kids had weed and arrested everyone. Even though he had nothing to do with possessing drugs, it was put on his record as drug trafficking. Silvia shared with me that this should have been an open and shut case.

The judge she spoke with in California agreed that the charges were bogus, but Homeland Security thought differently. Something that should have been over and done within a short time turned into a nightmare. Silvia and her husband first hired an attorney who took $10,000 of their money and submitted the wrong paperwork, making the case even more difficult. After hiring a new attorney, they fought for four years to help him get back to the U.S., but unfortunately, at some point, time was up, and he stayed in El Salvador.

They lost everything: their house, their cars, and all of their material possessions that they had both worked diligently for— sometimes working two jobs at a time. Silvia had to move in with her mother and share a room with her seven-year-old daughter. Her daughter became withdrawn and depressed. I have shared many conversations with Silvia over the last eight years, and what has continued to amaze me and give me chills every time I speak with her about it is the fierce love she and her husband have shared through it all. Her husband has had an unwavering faith the entire time that he will be reunited with his family on U.S. soil and that there will be a day when they will be living together here in Colorado again.

I have wondered at how she has found the strength to handle this. Many people would have already given up on ever having their spouse return and would have filed for divorce instead of dealing with the pain of having to live without their loved one. It has been very rough at times; It would have been easier for Silvia to give up, but she has remained in the daily practice of opening her heart when it wants to close, being in contact with her husband when she can, and continuing to visualize a future together.

They have fought for their love for the last eight years. They have kept the flame alive and fanned it, though only seeing each other once a year when Silvia travels to El Salvador with her daughter. They speak their fears, seek outlets to keep communication flowing; they've had difficult conversations, and have spoken their deepest truths to one another. Through tremendously punishing circumstances and painfully difficult challenges, they have continued to love each other fiercely through it all. When I run into Silvia, she reminds me of how loving fiercely is a conscious daily choice she is making. It is an intention to focus on what connects them and not what keeps them apart.

Sometimes, loving fiercely means we must sit with the fear that has risen in our hearts. Instead of getting busy, distracting ourselves, or being in denial as to how much it hurts, loving fiercely involves being with all of our emotions as they come up. It takes strength and courage to be with our fear and to keep our hearts open when everything in us is shouting, "Run!" or "Fight!" or "This feels dangerous!"

When the easy thing would be to shut down, fierce love calls for us to pull up what is resilient within us and to stay open—to acknowledge the pain and fear and to remain open hearted—because love is the ultimate healing balm.

When we are called to face our fear and allow ourselves to sit with it and not avoid it, we can drop out of the mind and the story we are carrying and into our bodies to see where we are holding that energy. As stated in the last chapter, when we breathe into those places in our bodies, we find we can breathe through the fear, and letting it go, we transcend it. When this happens, we find a reservoir of love in our hearts that is stronger than any circumstance.

Fiercely Loving Ourselves

We have all heard the phrase, "Just love yourself; be your own best friend." But I can attest that after thirty years in the mental health and personal development field, it isn't that easy. People don't just flip a switch and fall in love with themselves. I liken it to developing a friendship. When meeting someone, there isn't a conversation or two and then complete trust. It isn't normal, natural, or even healthy to say, "Well now that we barely know each other, I am going to trust you with my deepest, darkest secrets, and by the way, would you start picking up my toddler from daycare?" That would be absurd! It is no different when we are cultivating a relationship with ourselves. We must grow the trust that gives us a knowingness that we *can* depend on ourselves to have our own back.

I have gotten to experience this firsthand with my current partner. When we met, he told me about a spiritual quest he had been on twelve years before and that he had to leave Central America earlier than planned because he had gotten the news that his father was dying. He returned home and had six weeks with his father before he passed away from terminal cancer. He never got to finish his quest. I knew that going back to finish this quest was an essential part for him that would be happening at some point during our relationship. Family and friends didn't fully understand it and would question how I could possibly deal with him leaving me for an unknown amount of time to go back to Central America and finish his trip.

We have all heard the old saying, "When you love something, set it free," but to practice that saying is something entirely different. Not knowing how long he was going to be gone–anywhere from a month to three months–put my mind into a fight or flight state at times. Because our brain loves predictability, his being gone for an unknown amount of time felt like he had just been thrown into the abyss where I absolutely felt abandoned with no sense of control.

This was NOT easy! Even though I fully trusted him and believed in his mission, it brought up every hurt and trigger I had experienced by the abandonment of my father. There were times I felt I had lost my ground and had panic attacks in the middle of the day. Amidst twelve to fourteen-hour workdays, I was trying to manage out-of-control thoughts, which led to experiencing a wide gamut of emotions, and I felt completely overwhelmed. I would have a good day where I was back in balance meditating, exercising, and connecting with friends, and then the old message of, "You're just not important," would sneak back in.

This felt unbearable at times for two reasons. First, I had done a TON of work around the issue with my father and didn't believe (or even know) I still had so many layers to heal, and secondly, it was hard to witness myself falling into old behavior patterns, inactive for half my life, of wanting to shut down and run away. Talk about having to become fierce!

To begin this healing process, I had to first go inside myself. I had inner dialogues with parts of myself reminding me that even if no one else could see me, affirm me, or think that I was special, the divine always saw me, and I had a sacred connection to an infinitely unconditional source of love. I practiced daily, feeling into my heart and breathing there. I began to notice and attune to times when my heart would begin to shut down out of fear, and again, I would breathe room into it encouraging it to expand. This daily (sometimes, hourly) practice kept my heart open, and I could disconnect from the old story I was telling myself that was creating more anxiety and a need for protection.

One of the most powerful things I experienced was during a meditation group where the leader had us repeat phrases that our subconscious mind might be holding. As we unearthed the thoughts, we were then able to feel how they were connected to our bodies and how we were holding the energy within.

About halfway through the session, as our leader began a set of sentences, she paused and said, "Stephanie, this is for you." Surprised, I tuned in even more deeply as she asked us to repeat, "I... tell myself...I don't care...as a way of protecting myself... and not deal with my fear.... I tell myself... It doesn't matter... and trick my mind into thinking I don't care... so I can detach... and not have to feel the fear I am terrified to feel."

As she continued with these sentences, my body shook, my head became light, and I had a heightened awareness of this being the truth of my subconscious mind—the part of me that had kept my heart closed and protected. As I breathed through these sentences and began to release the energy from my body, I could feel my whole-body tingling, getting lighter. We finished the series with the words, "I now release these beliefs on all levels and let go of this on all planes now." Something inside of me shifted and there was more space for love and light to get through.

As I began to heal, I noticed I had deeper levels of compassion for my partner, his experience, and his feelings on his quest. I showed up fully present to our conversations and allowed grace, understanding, and support to be my guides. I breathed into the fire of love that I held for him and allowed the oxygen of our love to stoke the flames. There were days I practiced just being in-love with him, even when we had no contact, and I had no idea where in the world he was. I released the illusion of having control and the need to control anything in the relationship and just let myself love him fiercely. This enhanced not only my love for him, but also my love for myself. As I surrendered the relationship to the divine and allowed my love to flow freely through my heart, the feeling of loving him fiercely was abundant, and I regained my sense of peace, being fully grounded and more completely alive. We were meant to love in this way.

In reflecting on this time, I realized that I went through what Elizabeth Kübler Ross described in the five stages of grief. When my partner left, I was angry at him. I was caught up in my own issues of abandonment and even though I absolutely intellectually understood the reason he was going on his journey, the wounded little girl inside of me was very triggered and feeling abandoned. I went through the stage of bargaining... "Maybe he *isn't* the right guy for me?" and "If only this or that were different, I could be happy." And then the sorrow. I cried and cried and then I cried some more.

Rivers came out of me for all of the tears I had never released and for the pain I had never let surface before. And then, acceptance. Surrender to what is.

The ultimate freedom in letting go allowed me to reclaim

my life and to fall in love with it more deeply. I also grew more deeply in love with myself and my own unique expression and experience in this world. I learned how to love from a deeper place inside that did not require someone else to validate me. I became the embodiment of love, internally and externally. All my relationships blossomed as a result of it.

This journey through the pain to greater love, helped me reclaim lost parts of myself. One night, as I sat on my back porch, these words came through me, in what I call a "download"—one stream of consciousness that captured this journey for me perfectly:

Tonight, as I sit on my favorite swing,
under a magically lit porch,
the soothing sound of crickets,
which always takes me back to childhood summers,
fills the air, and my heart is full.

What a huge time of growth,
self-reflection,
and continued spiritual awakening.
I have learned so much about myself
through these past few months.
I have journeyed
to the depth of my soul,
experienced the scared,
scarred, and lonely little girl
that had set up camp
in a part of my soul
I had locked securely away...
now fully exposed...
raw...

awakening...

I have tried to deny she existed at all.
All the multiple times I've run from her,
all of the desperate distractions I've used at length,
to prove she wasn't there...
inevitably led me back to her trembling self...
eyes held wide with fear....
aching...
aching...
like a primal scream caught in the throat.
Abandoned.
Alone.

So, so afraid to love...
to be loved.
And then the awareness,
like a bullet through my heart:
It was not the outside world that had abandoned her...
It was me.
It was I, who left her so long ago...
told her she wasn't good enough to love...
screamed at her that she would never be enough...
*that she **could** never be enough...*
that she couldn't count on anyone....
I taught her in repetitions,
she could
Never.
Count.
On me.

For the last 40 years,
I have walked the earth
wishing
she would disappear,
or even die...
I didn't want her to be a part of me.
She didn't fit my Molly Brown image...
my joy-filled life I'd created...
I never wanted her to rear her tormented head...
to make things messy.
It took me this experience of outer circumstances
which induced a heartache that ripped me open
and shredded me to my core,
to reclaim her,
to allow her to surface again
from this lonely place where
I had denied her breath.

She did not let me avoid her this time.
She came out of the shadows, full force, with a vengeance.
She flooded my tear-rimmed eyes,
my heart and mindscape.
I could not escape her.

After the fury
and a bitter-shed oceans of tears,
and a gutting
that seemed to rip away the parts of me
I had held as reliable friends,

the smoke cleared,
and she was standing there
in a pure gown made of starlight.

For the first time,
since she came into existence,
I learned how to hold her deeply,
to hold onto
this orphaned part of myself
so tenderly and lovingly.

I held her
and I listened
and I listened
and I listened,
as she began to whisper
herself back to life.

Compassion soared through my veins,
and I held her more tightly
for all the years I had neglected her.

I spoke her name...
Beauty.

I breathed my love
into the very cells of her being
and watched the color and magic
return to her eyes,
her lips,

Her trust and tenderness flowing
in a perfect figure eight between us...
One fortifying the other...
Merging into one.

I feel her with me now. As me.
She has arisen from the dead
and shaken off the ashes
I had buried her with,
to fully inhale
this affirmation of life,
as healed breath
within my lungs.

I remind her daily,
"I've got you."
"You're mine."
"I will take care of you."
"You.
Are.
Loved."

Tonight, I surrendered her to the full moon;
not to say goodbye,
but to allow her to be
bathed in the moonlight
and return to me...
pure,
whole,
renewed

with a sense of wonder.

Had I not had my heart broken open,
she would have stayed in the shadows...
broken...

Tonight,
she is the firelight that dances before me
in the candle's wick,
she is the song of summer
that surrounds me
in a blanket of lullabies
that soothes my soul in
ancient melodies.

I have journeyed to the end of my soul
and when I looked out into the abyss...
I was the one there waiting....

Goddess,
Universe,
Pure love, staring back.
Transformed.

Take a Moment

One beautiful technique for cultivating this self-love is a meditation you can begin right now. Close your eyes and imagine a time when you were truly loving towards someone else. Picture their face, their eyes, their smile as you did or said loving things to them. Feel into your heart and notice how it radiates with the love you sent to that person. Take a deep breath in and really connect to your heart space.

Now recall a time when someone was truly loving towards you. Remember the words they said to you. Remember their kind gestures. Soak it in. Let that feeling fill up and radiate through your heart.

Breathe in.

Now, with both hands on your heart, feel into that space again. Allow yourself to start radiating that same sense of love to yourself that you have given to others. Start sending a sense of love to those parts of yourself that are already easy to love. It may be your sense of humor, or what a great friend you are. It may be the way your eyes sparkle or how you truly feel a connection with animals or nature. Take a careful inventory and send love to all the inner places that are already easy to love and marinate on that for a few moments.

Now imagine a love greater than yourself. This may be your higher self, the divine, the universe, or nature; imagine a sense of powerful unconditional love streaming in a beautiful light (in whatever color you associate with love) and feel it coming directly into the top of your head and streaming through to the parts of yourself you find more difficult to love. This may be your shame, or things about yourself you may have rejected, or your shadow side. Whatever it may be, imagine an unconditionally loving presence wrapping itself around those parts of you and infusing them with love. Notice how those parts of you respond when they are loved. Begin to open your heart even further as you say to yourself, "I am willing to be open to loving the parts of myself I have not yet been able to love." "I am willing to grow in love with myself."

This is where our fierce flame starts and is such a powerful process to cultivate a loving relationship with yourself.

When we truly love ourselves, we look at and handle life in a totally different way. Life begins to feel easier because we allow love to flow *to* us and *through* us and this is the kind of love that can change the world.

When we love ourselves, our heart is softened, and we show up in the world in a different way. We are more tolerant, more empathetic, and more compassionate. We become less critical and more accepting of others as we become less critical and more accepting of ourselves. We feel more peace, enjoy our own and others' company more fully, and we begin to look at the world through a different lens.

Imagine how this might truly impact the world. As we allow more love in, we radiate more out to everyone around us. Learning to love yourself is a powerful decision. Seeing the change we want to see in the world starts within each one of us.

FIVE

Finding Your Inner Roar

At the top of your lungs, shout and listen to the echoes.
You must live life at the top of your voice!

Ray Bradbury

How often do we speak what's on our mind or heart? How do we communicate in a way where we let our authentic selves show through? Part of becoming fierce is finding that inner voice and not just speaking the inner truth but also embodying it. Walking the talk and living in alignment with our highest self is how we inhabit this earth fully empowered. How do we go beyond just knowing our truth, to the full expression of it?

Big Examples

Sarah Edmondson devoted over a decade of her life to being extensively trained in a large company that turned out to be a sinister sex cult. In my lengthy interview with her, she expressed her involvement in the NXIVM cult, led by sociopath Keith Raniere. Sarah discussed the scars that were left on her, literally, from being branded by other cult members, and the emotional scars she has begun to heal. The subject of the HBO series, *The Vow*, Sarah describes the way she was manipulated and brainwashed, then where she found her strength to speak out, and finally, the long road of recovery. Strong and resilient, Sarah was eventually the whistleblower who helped put Keith Raniere under investigation, and ultimately, in a prison cell where he is currently serving 120 years. She got to a place inside of herself where the truth could no longer be silenced and had to be expressed in words and actions.

What was mind-blowing was how absolutely normal Sarah was. Smart and well-educated, she thought she was working for a company that was promoting self-development. By posing as a multi-level marketing company, NXIVM offered personal and professional development seminars to large groups through its Executive Success Programs. Unfortunately, it used many helpful therapeutic techniques to ultimately brainwash and completely manipulate members and, over time, to gain control over their lives.

It was chilling in the interview when Sarah said to me, "Stephanie, the thing is, if I had met you while I was still in the cult, I would have totally tried to convert you. Your vibrancy and positivity were exactly the qualities of the members we were looking for."

When I think about how Sarah had no idea that she was in a cult until the very end, I realized, ANY of us could get caught up in something like this if we didn't listen to our inner selves, or if we kept our truths and that inner voice quiet when the questions started coming up. That is exactly what Sarah had done to herself. She tried to rationalize and deny all the intuitions she kept getting. A deep need to belong and the incredible manipulation by others in the cult kept her inner voice quiet and dulled.

When she finally realized she had to get out, it took amazing strength to reach out to others in the cult that she could trust and to eventually blow the whistle and testify, which ultimately helped to bring the NXIVM cult down. This is an extreme example of finding the inner roar, and such a significant one. By speaking up and speaking her truth, Sarah saved thousands of others from experiencing the same horrific fate.

Years in recovery, she continues to use her voice to speak out and educate others by helping people to recognize and leave cult groups. Sarah is a powerful example of what can happen when we find our inner roar: we find ourselves, and we find the power to do what it takes to live in alignment and thrive.

NOT JUST FOR WOMEN

About 35 percent of my clients are men. Over the last fifteen years, in working intimately with them and exploring the interiors of their hearts, I have grown a depth of understanding in what many men struggle with. Finding your inner roar is not just a societal or inner dynamic unique to females. My clients have ranged from brain surgeons, CEOs, department chairs at universities, railroad workers and engineers, to pastors, a porn star, and a fireman who was a first responder at the Oklahoma City bombing at the daycare center. They have all struggled at times with finding their voice, their power, and allowing their fierce nature to be fully embodied and alive.

When Jim walked in the door, he appeared to take up the whole frame. He was 6'4" with broad shoulders and hands that enveloped mine as we greeted; I could see how it would be easy for him to be an intimidating presence to people. He was an officer in the U.S. Army and had been involved in overseas missions to Iraq and Afghanistan. Everything from his voice to the way he sat forward on the edge of his seat as he spoke, showed an exterior of strength. When we began to dig deeper into why he had come to see me, he revealed a very different interior. He shared a deeply wounded side, a side that had been told by a verbally abusive father that he could never do anything right and that he would never amount to anything.

He recalled a time as a little boy when he was watching his father change the oil in the family car. Jim's dad asked him to grab a wrench and as he did, he bumped against the oil pan, spilling a drop. His father grabbed the wrench out of his hands and threw it across the garage. "Don't fucking move!" He had shouted, "You are such an idiot!!"

Jim was six.

He grew up a people pleaser for fear of doing anything wrong. The Army was his escape from his interior fear that he was flawed and incompetent and his outer physical self became his protective shell from the wounds he carried within.

In relationships, he chose women who would reinforce this message of not being good enough. Despite his tough-looking exterior, he desperately just wanted to be loved and wouldn't speak up if he felt wounded or afraid in his relationships. Even when he found out his wife was having an affair, Jim was still trying to earn her love and not upset her. The affairs continued and Jim continued to internalize the hurt, anger, and betrayal and became more and more depressed and unhealthy.

After three failed marriages, he was ready to do the work to face whatever his demons were and to heal the little wounded boy inside of him.

Even though he could bark out orders to the enlisted men, his inner roar had been silenced. Early on, Jim had squelched the fire inside of himself, and the sparks of his essence were covered up and muted. He felt little happiness and had not experienced spontaneous joy since he was four or five years old. We began the work of excavating this spark and igniting the true lion that was inside of him.

Jim spent a little over a year in serious therapy, excavating everything he found. Layers of childhood trauma revealed a life not yet lived. Negative limiting beliefs were brought into the light and transformed. In addition to our time together, he used breathwork, and developed a devoted mindfulness practice. Over time and through great healing, we rescripted Jim's narrative. He began to find the words to express his feelings and to accept the realm of his inner experience, both the shadow side and the exuberant little boy who had been waiting to get out.

Jim's work involved weekly assignments of learning how to play. He joined an intramural basketball team and found out he loved being a part of a group that met at a local pizza place on Tuesday nights to play trivia games. He lightened up, he laughed more, and as he began to deeply heal, he met a new woman and began a relationship where he was able to be transparent and real with her. As their relationship continued, Jim described the long talks they had and how easily he could express himself, not only when things were going well, but more importantly, when he felt hurt, disappointment, and frustration in the relationship.

Jim became a fuller version of himself. He was more vibrant, more alive, and stronger than he had ever been. His inner roar finally matched his outer physicality, and his entire life became a reflection of this healing.

Witnessing his and others' healing continues as the greatest honors of my life.

As human beings we need to look at how we swallow our voice and what that does to our soul. Clients have described to me a slow soul death in relationships where they did not feel they could speak up and tell their truth because they strongly feared the reaction from their partner. This creates resentment, anger, anxiety, and depression. We are meant to speak our truths. Our souls cry out for freedom and expression. Our well-being and physical health depend on it.

The mind-body connection is so strong that when we begin to shut down emotionally, we can shut down physically as well. In doing so, we repress the immune system and then the unexpressed energy gets stored in the body, leading to disease. Just like we all need physical touch, we also need to be able to access our inner roar and our truth and to speak and express it.

WHEN THE HONEYMOON IS OVER

Years ago, I was in Cabo San Lucas with a man I loved. We

had been dating for about six months and were at a beautiful resort with several friends, having an amazing time snorkeling, swimming, and paddle boarding on the Sea of Cortez. On the third night there, we were all at a dinner party on the beach, hosted by my boyfriend's business partner.

There was a beautiful spread of food, tiki torches lit all around, live music, and sparkle lights strung between the trees. It was truly magical. When my boyfriend's business partner got up to speak at one point during the meal, a girlfriend of mine and I were in the middle of a hilarious story we were sharing and were laughing as he walked up to the microphone and began to speak. My boyfriend hushed us as we pulled ourselves together and tuned in. After his short speech, the evening went on just as magically as it had begun, and all was well... or so I thought.

The next morning as my boyfriend and I got ready to go on a whale watching cruise, he said something funny to me and I burst out laughing. He suddenly got very angry and said in a disgusted tone, "Why do you have to be so loud?!" He said it angrily and stomped into the other room. It was a flare of anger I had never witnessed.

I was instantly shamed. Huge, hot crocodile tears streamed down my face, and I was speechless. He did nothing to comfort me and just continued to get ready to go. Quietly, I got my things together to leave, but inside, I was disintegrating. This was a man who had told me from our first date how much he loved my exuberance, my lust for life, and my joy. He had shared how repressed he had been his whole life, always trying to just be the good kid and the golden child, and how it was hard for him to relax and just be himself. Of course, in the light of new love, his best self had been out those first six months. Grace, generosity, and tenderness were easier for him to access when he was flooded with the chemical cocktail of falling in love.

I was triggered back to being a child sitting at my grandparents' dinner table. "Be quiet. You need to sit still and not speak."

Shame from years of being silenced flooded me; all the years I had to swallow my voice and not speak up to a father that I desperately loved who I was no longer allowed a close relationship with; never being allowed to speak my truth and tell him how much my heart ached to have the fun and laughter we had once shared. Silenced out of that need for approval and some sort of connection, I had swallowed my voice again and again. The scab covering years of wounding was ripped off, and I could not regain access to my joy for the entire day. I watched the ocean from the whale boat feeling like something had died inside of me. My boyfriend didn't try to comfort me or connect. We both just sat on our opposite sides of the boat looking for giant tails to flip up in the water.

I was devastated.

That night I wrote down these words as a way of regaining my voice. Though I couldn't speak them yet, I had to gain access to my soul and locate my essence. I had to go beyond the trigger, to my truth.

Recently, I was told by someone that I have a loud voice
and that I laugh too loud.
I'm sorry if my joy and my exuberance for life
makes you feel uncomfortable
or puts you in touch with your own lack of authenticity.
I am not rude or obnoxious with my voice,
nor have I ever been a person that yells at others.
But I will not live my life in a "polite little box"
or minimalize my vibrancy
because women are meant to be seen and not heard.
I will not dim the shine on my soul
that finds expression in this world
so I can fit into someone else's mold

of what it means to be a lady.

I will not be silence or shushed
because you cannot tolerate
the unexpressed vibrancy
in yourself.

I will continue to shine, express, exude, emit, emanate, radiate,
and experience my joyful spirit
manifest in this world.
I will continue to bring
all the kindness, love,
and healing to this world
I can possibly muster.

I will continue to be
unapologetically myself.
Life wasn't meant
to be lived in muted tones
at volume two.
Life is meant
to be lived out loud.
Crank. It. Up.

The next morning, when I was able to fully inhabit myself and my voice again, I spoke to him about how hurtful his words and actions had been. I articulated what the triggers were for me and what wounds had been reopened. He had tears in his eyes and found empathy for my experience. He apologized and felt bad for hurting my feelings and we were able to move on, but our relationship was never the same. That moment was a window into our differences and how in the end, we were two very, very different people. The honeymoon was over.

We all have a need to be our vibrant, authentic selves. We have a deep desire to be loved and appreciated for our own unique self in this world. Finding my voice that day, internally and externally, was an empowering process. When we find our inner roar, it is not about yelling or shouting at one another; it is about owning our own experience and about being able to express it.

It is about being fully who we are.

SHOWING UP

I think it is important to note that part of discovering our inner roar is also about finding out what truly lights us up and makes us feel like the most authentic versions of ourselves. This might be expressed in the clothes we wear, make-up, tattoos, or what we choose to participate in, as well as what we choose to do in our career and during our leisure time. It's being unafraid to get in touch with the deeply playful, artistic, funny, inventive, spiritual, or intellectual sides of ourselves.

I have always loved the motto, "Keep Austin Weird," that is on T-shirts and mugs everywhere in that city, because it speaks to the importance of being our wild, unique, funky selves. It communicates the value of being different and that we don't have to give up these fantastic parts of ourselves to fit in. Austin flourishes on individuality and how that can create a vibrant vibe in a community and within a city. Think of how boring our gardens would be if we were only allowed to plant the same color of flower. Each one of our unique expressions is like a different colored flower in the world's garden, made more fragrant and beautiful by the combination of us all.

How would we act, show up, and express ourselves if we were unafraid to be fully ourselves? As long as our expression is not imposing on or hurting others, finding our inner roar is a call to our souls' freedom and to living a life in the fullness of what our divine spark was intended to be. I remember the words of Cat Stevens, "If you want to sing out, sing out, and if you want to be free, be free." What if we followed the melody of our souls and life became a beautiful rhythm we danced our way through with abandon?

We live in a world that continues to promote conformity in many ways and it can feel intimidating to break out and let our unique selves shine. Imagine how fascinating the world would be if we allowed ourselves and others to truly be and express who we are. When we show up as our authentic selves, we give others the permission to do the same. From that place of allowing ourselves and others to be in authentic expression, it would be amazing to see what could happen. The transformation of the world would be astounding.

THE GIFT OF OUR STORY

Sam Cawthorn is one of those amazing people who instantly captivates you with his charisma, his warmth, and his exuding passion for life. Currently, Sam is one of the world's top motivational speakers, the CEO and Founder of Speakers Institute and Speakers Tribe, author of eleven books (five of which are international bestsellers), and he is both the Young Australian of The Year and the Edu-preneur of The Year. I had the privilege of meeting Sam when I interviewed him for my radio show, *The Spark*. We met on a video call, he in Australia, and I, in Colorado, but during the call, there was no distance between us. Sam is a person who lives with total presence.

His story is such a compelling one, because he had to overcome extreme challenges in his life. Sam grew up in Tasmania. He was a shy kid and started mixing with a negative, toxic group of people and eventually got kicked out of and never finished high school. However, Sam knew there was something bigger that was meant to be in his life, so he began to surround himself with more positive people. He started a job for the Australian government as a youth futurist and life seemed to be going better.

That was until 2006, when Sam hit a semi-trailer truck head on and was pronounced dead at the scene.

He was resuscitated, on life support for a week, in the hospital for five months, and in a wheelchair for a year. Sam's right arm was amputated above the elbow, he suffered six broken ribs, collapsed lungs, and his leg was completely shattered. He spoke about the anguish of having his four-year-old daughter come to see him at the hospital for the first time and how worried he was that he would frighten her without his arm.

Instead, when his daughter entered the room, she hopped on his bed and said, "Daddy, did you have a car accident?"

Sam said, "Yes, I had a car accident."

"Daddy, did you lose your arm?" She inquired further.

"Yes, it's true, I lost it." Sam replied.

"Daddy, the doctors, they couldn't find your arm anywhere?!!"

She literally thought they just had to find Sam's arm so they could tape it back on! The absolute acceptance and love from his children, family, and colleagues, helped champion Sam's recovery physically, mentally, and emotionally, and he truly began to heal.

Sam said he remembered during that time, feeling that his own experience wasn't important because he was comparing it to a friend, who had lost an arm and a leg, in a shark attack. He said he later realized that we can't compare our story to anyone else's; we each have a unique voice and each one of our own experiences is important. The gift we can share is how when we understand the importance of our own story, we can then tell it in a way that can inspire others to rise up beyond their own challenges.

He talked about how there are celebrities that bore us after five minutes, and ordinary people who can make a trip to the grocery store sound like a cliff-hanging thriller. It was this awareness that totally changed his career. Sam realized he could craft his own story and get paid for telling it in a powerful way that made a difference in other people's lives. In the last fifteen years, Sam has been telling his story and inspiring international audiences, sharing the stage with Michelle Obama, Richard Branson, and the Dalai Lama, to name a few.

What a gift! Through his own experience, he is helping people see themselves, see their inner potential, and cultivate a knowing that their voice—their story—is important. Sam has also helped thousands of people find their inner roar through his Speakers Institute and his Speakers Tribe. Such a powerful process to bring stories to life and to give them wings!

Sam's message is that everyone has a story and that our stories are our number one trump card because each one of us has a story that is completely unique, beyond compare. It gave me a heightened awareness of how important it is to take time to discover our own stories within.

Take a Moment

Make a list of the important events in your life, the ones that challenged you, inspired you and the ones that helped define who you are as you overcame them. You might make a top five hits list, or if there is more, a top ten hits list. The list is only for you to briefly record the incident.

It might look like:

1. Moved in second grade.

2. Felt teased by others.

3. Parents' divorce.

4. Put myself through college.

5. Started living my passion through singing at a local club.

It's essential to know what challenges or circumstances created your story, but more importantly, what are the lessons you learned from each event?

On a separate sheet of paper, record the lessons learned from each experience. What was meaningful? What did you incorporate into your belief system? What was life changing for you? How is your life better because of it?

Even if you never choose to share your story or the wisdom gained from it, the exercise will help you to rediscover and reclaim these important parts of yourself and will give voice and value to your experience. How you choose to share it, is then up to you. You may find your inner roar again and other parts of yourself you may want to express more fully. You may be able to articulate your thoughts and feelings with others in a more confident way, or you might just find yourself on a podcast or a stage, inspiring others. It is an amazingly healing process to just acknowledge where you have come from and what is meaningful in your life.

Your story matters.

Set your voice free.

SIX

GATHERING STRENGTH

Continue. Be loving
And be strong. Be fierce and
Be kind. And don't give in
And don't give up.

Maya Angelou

We live in challenging times. No doubt. All one needs to do is turn on the news to be instantly transported into a world that looks fearful, discouraging, and catastrophic. Instantly, our fight or flight response can get activated as our brain screams to us, "Danger! Danger! Danger!" So how do we deal with these unpredictable and challenging times and a world that feels chaotic and beyond challenging?

The answer lies in learning to go within. There are two different types of control we can experience. Internal and external locus of control. When our sense of well-being is dictated by how people respond to us and by our outer circumstances and situations, we have an external locus of control. The problem with this, is that when we are externally controlled, life is unpredictable and scary, good one moment and horrifying the next. If it's a cloudy day, we are depressed, or if someone is rude to us, we are angry for the afternoon.

When something happens in the world, we move into a helpless state and feel overwhelmed. All of this can leave us in a state of misery. When we have an internal locus of control, the wind may howl, our car might break down, and governments may topple, and still, we hold an inner calm—a place of reserve where we can find our strength and be deeply grounded within.

One of my first experiences of this kind of groundedness happened in 2004, when my step- brother and his wife were in Sri Lanka during a tsunami. My parents called me that morning to tell me they hadn't heard from him and had no way of getting ahold of him. None of us knew that my stepbrother and his wife had actually been staying in a hotel right on the beach that was completely destroyed.

My anxiety was instantly ratcheting up along with concern over their safety, but my parents stayed calm as they spoke about it and continued to stay grounded all throughout the next two days, waiting to hear if he and his wife were dead or alive.

I remembered thinking, *How can they not be hysterical?!* If it were one of my daughters in the same situation, I couldn't imagine how I would be handling it without freaking out. When I inquired about how they were remaining so calm, they shared with me that they were concerned, but that there was nothing they could do besides pray for their safety and surrender the rest to God. They shared that they meditated twice a day to keep themselves centered. They said that the outcome was out of their control and that they were going on the information that was available to them.

If the worst had happened, of course they would be extremely sad, but that it didn't serve anyone if they were catastrophizing the situation and expecting the worst outcome. They were holding their center and holding a collective field of love and strength for my stepbrother and his wife and for one another.

Two days later, we got the news. Early in the morning, the

day the tsunami had hit, my stepbrother and his wife had woken up and discussed whether to take the train up the mountain to see the elephants and have their coffee that morning at the top of the mountain, or to stay in the hotel and have their coffee by the ocean.

They had decided to go ahead and take the train up the mountain; a decision that ended up saving their lives. I spoke to my stepbrother three days after the event, and he shared that they had no idea a tsunami was coming that morning. He told me about a moment during their ascent up the mountain when they passed another train full of passengers that was descending. As the train tracks were very close and ran side by side, he recalled seeing the smiling faces of the people in the other train and how everyone had waved to one another as the two trains passed. Lots of smiles and waves were shared.

My stepbrother and his wife didn't know until they had reached the top of the mountain that the tsunami had hit below and all of the passengers on the descending train had been killed.

It was a devastating and transcendent experience for them and a deep lesson for me. There was grief for the many, many people who lost their lives, and a huge lesson learned from my parents about how to hold on to ourselves as we are going through difficult circumstances. It wasn't about just being optimistic and thinking, "Oh, everything will be okay." It was a depth of holding on to oneself in the present moment, surrendering to a higher power, and not letting fear dictate our internal experience.

Powerful indeed.

A WAY THROUGH

One of my dear friends, Misa Hopkins, is an amazingly talented healer, bestselling author, and spiritual badass. She has been healing others for decades. We first met when I interviewed her three years ago and by the end, we were friends and felt moved to collaborate on projects together. She shared her Holding Meditation with me, and it became a lifeline during difficult times. In this meditation she asks the listener to go into the very core of themselves to find the divine light that is always holding them.

When I went through a painful break up, I listened to it every evening for months. Deeply grounding, it returned me to a place where I could hold onto myself, connect to the divine, and feel empowered within. It became a constant in my life when the external circumstances were changing and unpredictable.

Not only when our outer life is difficult, but at *all times,* having a daily practice to lean into builds strength within. It's like building a muscle. It is through repetition that the muscle is strengthened, and we can see the results. The same is true for our inner process. It reminds me of a mighty oak. The winds may howl, and the storms may blow the branches of the tree to and fro, but the core of the oak remains solid, its roots deep.

What creates the feeling of being grounded? Many clients I work with are going through life transitions: finishing graduate school and not finding a job or retiring and feeling overwhelmed and depressed.

One of the common factors I have found that helps my clients begin feeling like they are gathering strength again is establishing a routine, especially a morning routine. As simple as that sounds, the results are profound. Our brains love predictability and patterns. When life is uncertain, it can make our fight or flight response kick in and we experience anxiety. Planning the first hour of the day (even the first half an hour) can help the brain begin to calm down. It knows what to expect.

I also love the concept of "bookends" to the day, having a morning and evening grounding routine. We can prime our mind, body, and soul in the morning by asking ourselves just a few questions, such as:

"What are three things I am thankful for?"

"What is a positive message I most need to hear today?"

"What are three things that would make today really great?"

"If I showed up as my best self today, I would....?"

And then in the evening, taking a few minutes to journal:

"What was the best thing that happened today?"

"What would make tomorrow even better?"

"One person I want to send love to right now is...."

"Three things I am thankful for that happened today are..."

The power of this exercise is that not only does it prime the mind in the morning to anticipate having an amazing day (the subconscious mind is looking for the things already planted in it), but also it reinforces the positive thoughts and feelings in the evening that will be marinated upon subconsciously for the next seven, eight, or nine hours while asleep. This is a powerful feedback loop that will put the mind on the right track for optimal well-being.

Some other effective ways I have found to feel centered and gain inner strength is through movement, breathwork, meditation, and being in nature. These things bring our bodies and minds into a deeper state of connection with ourselves and with something bigger than us that can soothe our souls.

COMMUNING WITH NATURE

Research tells us that time in nature is an antidote for stress. It can lower blood pressure and stress hormone levels, reduce nervous system arousal, enhance immune system function, increase self-esteem, reduce anxiety, and improve mood. It is the perfect remedy for what ails us.

As I shared already, I have a morning practice of putting my bare feet on the earth each morning as I let my dogs out. Whether it is snowing, or the summer sun is just coming up, I step on the ground, raise my hands in the air, and soak up the sky. I listen to the birds singing and feel the wind on my face and connect to all that is. Taking a few breaths in, I also connect more deeply to myself, and feel profound gratitude for the beauty in each day. It is literally a touchpoint for me to step into my morning from a place of reverence for all of life and a way to jump start my day with a sense of well-being.

I was struck when one of my friends said his daily mantra was, "Look up." Look up! There is always something to notice in the sky, no matter what time of day it is: storm clouds, sunset, a rainbow, starlight; it is all magnificent and puts us in touch with something greater than ourselves. One of my favorite things to do is grab a bunch of blankets and some pillows and lie on the deck of my mom's cabin in Red Feather Lakes, Colorado. Under a new moon, watching shooting stars is breathtaking. I have spent many nights lying out there beneath a star-blanketed sky, talking and laughing with dear friends, and being in wonder at the magnificence dancing before us.

Try stopping and looking at the sky at any time of the day or night and notice how it affects the body and the mind. This is a simple process that helps to strengthen the sense of well-being and gives access to a portal of connectedness with the amazing world we live in.

We rely on nature. The plants, the sea, and the animals are all essential for food, water, and oxygen for us to survive and thrive. There is something magical that happens when we are in a deeper relationship to it.

As a scuba diver, I have often said that "heaven" is what is happening under the sea. For me there is no deeper way to commune with nature than being totally submerged in it.

One of my favorite dives is a site called Rodger's Backyard in Maui. A few years ago, I was in total awe as the divemaster chased an octopus from a coral reef. I watched with delight as the lovely creature propelled himself through the water, gliding like a graceful dancer until he reached another reef. In that moment, the octopus wrapped itself around the coral and instantly changed colors. I had no idea they were chameleons! It was absolutely thrilling and fascinating!

On that same dive, I came around another coral reef, only to find three giant sea turtles sitting on the ocean floor facing one another, looking like they were just hanging out having a conversation. I was so struck by this scene that I began to weep. At nearly six feet long and about 150 years old, the turtles made me feel small. I knew the immensity of the ocean, sensed the wisdom of their collected years, and was in awe of these three beings who had survived many storms and challenges of the sea to meet there together in total communion.

When we commune with nature, we are pulled into a deeper relationship with ourselves. There is evidence of something greater than ourselves as we join with the wisdom of the forest, the beauty of the ocean, or the sky in all of its splendor. We are part of this beautiful circle and when we connect to it, we can gather strength from it in the deepest parts of our being.

BREATHWORK

Wim Hof is a wild motivational speaker, extreme athlete, and is known as The Iceman for his ability to withstand freezing temperatures. He has set Guinness World Records for swimming under the ice and for prolonged full body contact with it. Born in the Netherlands, Wim developed a method that is a powerful way to activate and reawaken inner power through a combination of frequent cold exposure, breathing techniques, yoga, and meditation. I had the privilege of seeing him speak four years ago in New York City at a Tony Robbins event.

The breathwork he taught us at that event has been life-changing for me and has become a tool I have shared with my clients experiencing anxiety and panic. It consists of taking forty full, deep breaths into the lower part of the lungs and then exhaling rapidly, one after another. After the fortieth breath, the air is exhaled completely and then held for as long as possible.

Then another series of twenty breaths are done in this same manner, holding the twentieth after the exhale for as long as possible. Invigorating for the physiology, not only does it oxygenate blood, but it also excites the parasympathetic nervous system to result in calm and grounded feelings.

After the event, I was able to put this technique to the test when I was flying out of Newark. Thunderstorms had delayed the plane for thirty-five minutes. While on the runway, I spoke with the man sitting beside me, an MMA fighter, who had just returned from a fight in Egypt. He showed me the pictures of his swollen eye and injuries after his last fight. This guy was tough! Finally, the plane was given clearance and we were able to take off.

Never before or since, have I been in such a turbulent ascent. The plane was not just pitching up and down, but also side to side as we battled through the clouds. I observed my fight or flight response activating and the adrenaline and cortisol beginning to flow through my veins. Even though I could still logically say to myself, "Everything is going to be alright," my own physiology was saying something different.

I grabbed on the seat ahead of me to somehow feel I had a grip on something as the plane continued its tumultuous ascent, and I looked over at the MMA fighter beside me. He too, was gripping onto the seat in front of him for dear life. We made eye contact and started laughing as we both noticed our desperate holds on the back of the seats.

That was enough of a break in the fight or flight trance I was beginning to go into, to allow me to remember Wim Hof's breathing technique. I instantly began to do the forty breaths. The results were absolutely fascinating. The plane continued its bumpy ascent, pitching to and fro, but I was calm, quiet, and centered inside. My entire body relaxed, and my mind was at ease. This was a powerful lesson in knowing that we cannot always control our outer circumstances, but we can make a change from within that alters our entire experience. Our breath is a fierce ally in combating that which scares us.

Even ten deep, slow breaths will change the body's physiology. Our breath can help us gather strength in times of need and can also help build those muscles as a daily centering practice. The more we rely on the breath to help us return to a place of calm (and our inner locus of control), the more we are strengthening the internal muscle of memory, of routine.

Remember, the brain and mind like familiarity and predictability.

Our breath is a gateway to connecting to our inner resource of resilience.

MOVEMENT, EXERCISE, AND VITALITY

It is not enough to just survive this life. We can lead dynamic, empowered, and fantastic thriving lives. What is the secret recipe to living an amazing life? Move.

Move in any way that provokes feelings of vitality. Dance, run, do tai chi, kickbox, swim, jump on a trampoline, practice yoga, take long walks, skip down the street... just move. I always remember the saying, "A body in motion, stays in motion." When we get moving, we want more of it. It boosts our mood, improves our sex lives, combats disease and health conditions, increases energy, and promotes better sleep. Think of movement as the battery recharge of our lives. We have to plug in to keep working, thriving, and living at our best.

When I had Global Embodiment Coach and yoga superstar Cristi Christensen on my show recently, I was blown away by her abundant energy and effervescent vitality. By blending dance, yoga, and breathwork, she creates a kind of movement that awakens and ignites the energy inside. The amazing thing about Cristi is that her passion for movement comes from her own personal trauma. Growing up, Cristi suffered from multigenerational abuse and struggled with an eating disorder for over ten years. She found escape in gymnastics and dance, performing at the North Carolina School of Arts.

At sixteen, she transitioned to another movement passion,

platform diving. Cristi was an Olympic hopeful and trained with the U.S. Olympic diving team, but all of these dreams were shattered when she suffered a devastating back injury. Her spirit was crushed along with her dreams. Cristi then embarked on a spiritual journey of self-discovery and when a friend invited her to her first yoga class, it became a portal for her to awaken the fire within and heal herself on deeper levels. Movement became both her healer and the gift that she began to share with others to help ignite their awakening and healing process.

In our interview, she talked about the essential rituals we need to utilize to strengthen ourselves daily and candidly shared that she teaches this because she needs it too. It is her medicine. It is like a daily vitamin for all of us. In her new book *Chakra Rituals: Awakening the Wild Woman Within*, she focuses on awakening each of the energy centers inside of us. Imagine if we were a battery with all of these different energy cylinders inside. Imagine how much more powerful we would be if we were actually firing on all cylinders, if all of our being felt more awake and alive at each of these energy centers. What might we be capable of?

Another way of creating vitality in the body is through tapping. There is a process called Emotional Freedom Technique, or EFT. EFT is an evidence-based, self-help therapeutic technique that is highly effective in reducing the symptoms of depression and anxiety. It is similar to acupressure in that it works with acupoints on the body that stimulate the central nervous system and cause the body to release helpful chemicals. Tapping increases well-being and happiness, and significantly reduces symptoms of PTSD, depression, anxiety, and reduces pain in the body.

In EFT, a person uses the fingertips to stimulate energy in the body where it can get stuck. By tapping on the body's meridian points, this trapped energy can be released. We know that an imbalance of energy flow in the body can lead to immune problems and health issues. EFT is a way to release negative energy and tap further into vitality.

I have used it effectively in my own life and have seen the results of it with my clients for the last fifteen years. Clients with phobias, panic disorders, depression, and PTSD have all had significant relief from this technique.

I once had a client who was claustrophobic and unable to ride in elevators. Because she worked on the fifteenth floor, this fear was extremely time consuming and limiting for her, causing great distress.

After just three EFT sessions, we were able to test out how effectively the tapping was working by doing an actual experiment. The historic hotel across the street from my office has a very small elevator with an antique-looking metal gate that shuts before the doors close. Before EFT, when my client thought of being in an elevator, her anxiety spiked.

After utilizing EFT tapping, we shut the metal doors of the elevator and as the outer doors closed, I looked at her to see a smile on her face and relief in her eyes. She joyfully exclaimed, "I've got my life back!"

Not only were we able to totally alleviate her fear of being in elevators, but EFT also gave her a lifelong tool she could use to help in those moments when life got stressful, and she felt stuck. To give you an idea of how EFT can work in your life, you can try it in the Take a Moment at the end of this chapter.

LEANING IN

Although it may feel counterintuitive, leaning into the places where we feel weak and vulnerable is actually a powerful way of gathering strength. We don't gather strength by running away. We gather strength by leaning in and acknowledging the places that scare us: our fears, insecurities, and sorrows. When we try to hide those parts of ourselves, we are weakened because we have a fear that those parts might be exposed. We fear that our imposter complex will become a reality and people will find out we aren't the exterior fortress we are trying to portray. It takes courage to step inside these places and embrace and welcome them instead of rejecting and hiding those aspects of ourselves.

I have a core transformation process I do with clients where I have them drop directly into those parts of themselves. If a person is noticing they are triggered repeatedly by something in their life, we first define what the emotion or reaction is, and then explore the part of them that is experiencing that emotion. By floating back in their timeline, they discover how old that part is, and then feel into their body to sense where that part "lives" and where that emotion shows up for them.

The process is a beautiful uncovering of that part of themselves which leads to welcoming and receiving the part. Instead of rejecting this part when it is activated by some negative external circumstance, this part is given a voice. I ask my clients to connect with their part and ask, "What do you want?" and then listen for a response, or a body sensation, or an image to appear. What is amazing is that the parts of us that are fearful, or anxious, or insecure, actually want a deeply positive outcome for us. They just don't know how to go about getting it. Often, they are trying to protect us and keep us from harm, but our emotional shut down, or continued negative experience of emotion is perpetuated instead.

We all have core states that we desire: love, wholeness, a sense of oneness, and peace. Our emotions and behaviors are either adaptive or maladaptive ways of getting to these core states. The irony is, we don't have to "do" anything to earn these core states, we just have to open up and allow our wounded parts to step into a core state and experience it in the now. When we befriend those parts of ourselves by holding and really listening to what they want for us and then thank them for truly wanting the best intended outcome for us, we are able to help those parts transcend, transform, and integrate with our present self. We allow that part to heal, and we become more fully healed in the process.

When I lead this transformation process, I have clients imagine their timeline stretching out behind and in front of them with an awareness of themselves in the present moment.

Then, they imagine they can float up over their timeline, all the way back to just before the moment of their conception and drop into that exact time. Then I invite them to imagine the core state (such as love) that their part ultimately wants for them to have at every moment of their lives moving forward.

They imagine their lives then fast forward in time to the present and then again out into their future, infusing each moment, consciously and unconsciously with their core state fully present, coloring, penetrating, and permeating each experience and their entire lives. This is a powerful process which teaches how we can truly gain internal strength by listening to and befriending the parts of us we hide or are uncomfortable with and help them transcend into a more fully integrated ally in our journey through life.

We can also lean in by moving towards, rather than away from, what scares us. Think about it. If there is a strong sense of fear of public speaking, that vulnerability might manifest anxiety in even the thought of stepping up to a microphone. What if, instead, we learn to lean into the vulnerability, commit to practice, or hire a coach until we master feeling confident being on stage or speaking on a microphone; that same vulnerability and great fear could become just the energy needed to motivate action!

Ironically, when we share our vulnerabilities with trusted others, we gain strength as well. We no longer have to hide who we are. We give ourselves permission to be imperfect, and are able to show up more authentically ourselves, more fully empowered.

There is a myth that there are successful people who have it all figured out. No one does! As long as we are breathing, there will be challenges, triggers, and vulnerabilities that arise. Embracing them, digging deeper, and learning how to respond to them in a way that requires stepping into and owning oneself completely is actually the alchemy needed to transform them.

HOW THIS RELATES TO FIERCENESS

This chapter might bring up thoughts like Well, those are all pretty gentle ways of gathering strength. I thought being fierce would be a more forceful approach.

We become fierce just like an Olympic athlete becomes the best in the world: through practice. We build our own inner strength by taking care of ourselves in holistic manners and through these daily practices of meditation, mindfulness, breath work, exercise, and our connection with nature that build an inner fortitude which will sustain us through all of life's difficulties. When the rest of the world is feeling chaotic and is overwhelming, we can be that calm eye of the storm within.

I am in the middle of doing the 75 Hard challenge. It is a seventy-five day mental toughness commitment consisting of two forty-five minute daily workouts (one inside and one outside, regardless of the weather), eating a healthy diet with no cheat meals, drinking a gallon of water, and reading ten pages a day. I have done yoga outside in a rainstorm and worked out late at night when I would have rather been sleeping, but I am committed to this process. If I mess up or miss anything at all, I have to start back over at day one. This kind of challenge builds grit, resiliency, and commitment in a powerful way. It teaches that when we can overcome difficult challenges day to day, we can take on the bigger challenges in life; we build that inner muscle of fortitude to face the bigger storms. We become fierce.

When we gather our own inner strength, we become beacons of lights for others who are trying to find their way. We become the lighthouse that helps others navigate through their storms safely. It takes courage to become our own source of well-being. It takes strength to build self-worth from the inside out. It takes guts to dive into the inner-self and explore what's there.

On the entrance to the Parthenon the words, "Know Thyself" are inscribed. Could this be the secret code to true strength and our ability to show up as fierce, fully empowered beings?

When we have resourced ourselves and built this inner alliance, we become a force to be reckoned with because we no longer need the rest of the world to show us who we are. When we gather strength in these ways, we can rely on ourselves and know we have the internal resources to be a fierce being in this world. We can show up fully and authentically who we are.

Take a Moment

I want you to experience for yourself how EFT may work in your life. First of all, think of something that is disturbing you. It can be a negative emotion, or an unpleasant memory of a person, place, or thing that evokes a negative response. Before tapping, come up with a phrase of what is bothering you. For example, "Fear of speaking in meetings."

Next, find the two pressure points just about four inches below your collarbone on each side. You will know when you have found these points because there are two lymph nodes there and it is a little tender. Next, begin rubbing these points and say out loud, "Even though I have a fear of speaking in meetings, I deeply and completely accept myself." Repeat this three times.

While repeating your fear (as in our example) "Fear of speaking in meetings," use your fingertips to then tap five to seven times each on nine of the body's meridian points: top of the head, inner eyebrow, side of the eyes, under eyes, under nose, middle of the chin, under collar bone, under armpit, and the karate chop point (this is the point at the center of the fleshy part of the outside of either hand, between the top of the wrist and the base of your pinkie finger, where you would actually give someone a "karate chop").

Go through all points and then notice how you feel. If there is still some disturbance left, return to the lymph nodes under the collarbones and rubbing them again in a circular motion say three times, "Even though I still have a fear of___, I deeply and completely accept myself." Go back through the tapping sequence, using your phrase each time you tap on a meridian.

Then, I like to go through the tapping sequence again, utilizing a positive phrase I want to "tap in." Using the above example, I might say something like, "I feel confident speaking in all situations," or "I can easily speak my truth."

After tapping in the new thoughts, notice how you feel. You can go through the positive tapping sequence several times and feel it amplifying as it is being more hardwired into your system.

Tapping sends signals directly to the stress centers of the midbrain, thus reducing the stress or negative emotion that is connected to the thought and can help repair any energy disruption and ultimately restore balance to your being. This is a powerful way to gather strength and overcome your anxieties and fears, which allows you to show up in the world in a bold, fierce, and beautiful way.

SEVEN

PURGE WHAT DOESN'T SERVE

Close your eyes and imagine the best version of you possible.
That's who you really are,
let go of any part of you that doesn't believe it.

C. Assaad

For over thirty years, I have worked intimately with individuals from all walks of life. I started out working with adolescents in psychiatric hospitals, then worked with geriatrics and developmentally delayed individuals. From there, I ran a cognitive behavioral therapy treatment program for the seriously mentally ill, working mostly with individuals with paranoid schizophrenia. I then spent a decade working for a school district working with elementary school children and their families at a school with a 73 percent poverty rate population, and for the last fifteen years I have been working in my private practice with individuals and couples, and with those suffering from PTSD, as a trauma specialist. All this to say, I have seen A LOT of life.

There have been many common threads throughout this career that I have seen as either tripping cords for people's growth and development, or the golden threads that helped propel them to greater states of being, expanded their joy, and empowered them in ways they never thought possible. For many, it is their inability to let go of old belief systems, toxic people, relationships, or their personal "story" that keep them stuck. I have also worked with individuals that were so over-invested in acquiring material possessions, that they believed somehow helped define them or gave them a sense of value, that they became prisoners to these things outside of themselves as markers of their inherent worth.

How do we let go of these threads that become the chains that bind us? How do we create a life where we are fierce and lit up individuals living our lives in full expression? From holding on to grudges, resentments, and a victim mentality, to becoming fierce in the world requires us to let go of the people, places, attitudes, beliefs, and things that no longer serve us. We must learn the art of the purge so our souls can be fully free.

When Beliefs Go Bad

My Uncle Lloyd told me a story once that struck me profoundly. His description of a transformative experience highlighted how powerful our beliefs and perceptions are. It started on his way home from Denver, driving on I-25. He said as he drove back to Fort Collins that spring day, he noticed that it had begun to rain as he headed north out of the city. He had just finished a workshop and was happily buzzing in his mind and body about all he had gathered and learned that day. As he continued his journey, he started to notice people pulling off to the side of the road. The rain was getting heavier, but still he continued, feeling exuberant from his day. As he drove, he noticed more and more cars pulling off under the overpasses. At one point, another driver came alongside him and started honking his horn urgently. As my uncle looked over, the man was yelling at him and pointing desperately at his windshield. It was at that moment, my uncle looked directly at his windshield and noticed that he had never turned on his windshield wipers and realized how amazingly hard the rain was coming down, and like all of the other drivers, had to immediately pull over because at that moment, he could no longer see through the storm.

What changed? The rainstorm had not gotten any heavier. It was his perception of the rainstorm that had changed. When he thought he could see and was happily on his way home, all was well. The instant that he was reminded to turn on his windshield wipers, his vision completely changed, and he was no longer able to continue his journey.

How curious that we may have these misperceptions in our lives, ways that keep us focusing on the storm instead of the clear view that is also available to us. Oftentimes, we see the storm: what isn't working, the coworker that is creating havoc in our lives, the miscommunication with our partner, the lack of income or opportunity we experience, the negative beliefs we hold about ourselves, or the resentments about what we feel others have done to us. All of this keeps us stuck. All of this causes us to be pulled over to the side of the road, unable to continue our journey because we can't see clearly to travel ahead.

How do we become the clear conduits in our lives for more energy, joy, resiliency, peace, and connection? We must look deeply at our lives and purge what doesn't serve.

PURGING BELIEFS

Like my uncle's experience, we can hold on to certain beliefs that guide our behavior and how we show up in the world. We can know that any limiting belief we hold is truly keeping us from experiencing ourselves and the world in the expanded capacity available to us.

"As he thinks, so he is; as he continues to think, so he remains." Wise words from James Allen in his book, *As a Man Thinketh*. What we think about directly affects how we feel, how we act, and how we manifest our reality in the world. The more we think certain thoughts, the more they become ingrained into a belief system that begins to define how we see ourselves and how we view others, and directly dictates how we experience ourselves in the world.

It's cognitive-behavioral therapy 101: Changing thoughts will change feelings, which in turn changes actions and directly affects an individual's experiences of life. At one point, in the recent past, I caught myself saying, "I never have enough time for all the things I have to do." I had been saying it to myself for months with deadlines for my film, radio show, and events I was putting on, along with a full private psychotherapy practice, and book writing demands. And yes, that is a lot AND if that is the mentality and the belief that I hold on to, I will NEVER find time because my belief system supports that there is always a lack of it, and I will end up feeling anxious and more stressed.

What was interesting, is that when I became aware of this repetitive thought in my head around not having enough time, I decided I could consciously do something about it to change that pattern. I took a look at all of the things I had going on in my life and was able to look at where I was wasting time and eliminate some of the activities and engagements I had put on my plate that weren't essential pieces to my well-being and happiness. I quit a women's group, an over-commitment that I wasn't resonating with. I started meditating for twenty minutes during my lunch break and being intentional about the people I wanted to connect with on a social and professional basis; then, things immediately started to shift. I felt spaciousness, downtime, the exhale of coming back more fully into my body, and grounding with a rhythm that was more aligned with my soul.

Now, I make it a part of my morning and evening routine to affirm my intention to be grounded, and have clarity, connection, and spaciousness. What was once a negative mantra, "I never have enough time," has been replaced with, "Time is on my side. I can relax into the flow of this day, this moment."

Time didn't change. My perception of it, my relationship with it, and what I focused on for the day changed, and my well-being and productivity increased greatly.

When we start to see the cracks in the beliefs that don't serve us, we can ask ourselves three questions:

1. Is this an absolute big "T" Truth, or is it something I have just said to myself so many times I believe it is true?

4. How is this belief serving me? And if it's not, am I willing to let it go? When?

5. What would I like to believe about myself instead?

When we become aware of what we would like to believe about ourselves instead of the old belief that is not really true and does not serve us, we can implement the new belief the same way we unconsciously created the other negative belief: through repetition. Allow this new belief to become the new mantra. For thirty days, write it down and at the end of the day, write down all of the evidence that showed up to support this new belief. What we focus on expands and we will begin to see evidence of the new belief in our life.

PURGING POSSESSIONS

In her book, *The Life-Changing Magic of Tidying Up,* Marie Kondo teaches about the Japanese art of decluttering and organizing. There was a particular chapter about the clothes in our closet that always stuck with me. How many times have I purchased something that looked good at the moment, and it hung in my closet for months (or years!) and I never ended up wearing it? Or, I'd get something for a special occasion and then wear it once, and then it took up space in my closet (and in my life).

I have had times when my closet was packed and I thought, "I have nothing to wear!" Talk about first-world problems! When our closets are packed and full of things we no longer want, wear, or feel good in, it is like we have energetically cluttered our lives. No new energy (or outfits) can fit in that stuffed closet. It is time to purge.

Marie suggests touching each item and asking, "Does this bring me joy?" and if not, to get rid of it. This can be such a pleasurable process. I love giving clothes to my mom, sister-in-law, and sister, and donating the rest. It has become a biannual ritual for us, and such a fun way to share what no longer is sparking joy in my life and such a pleasure to watch it spark joy with the other women in my family. We always share a secret smile when one of them shows up to the next family event in one of my outfits looking amazing!

The book goes on to encourage the reader to do this purging process with everything in their home, room by room, until all that is left are the things that they truly love. We know from quantum physics that everything is energy and the subatomic particles that make up everything in our universe hold energy. If we are holding on to things that no longer bring us joy, we are holding on to energy that does not serve our lives. We are clogging up our ability to be clear conduits for ideas, inspiration, and divine energy to come through. Just start with one room, one drawer, and notice how feelings shift after this process. It is truly empowering.

It's like taking a deep breath and a long exhale that leaves us feeling lighter, more refreshed, and grounded. Giving it away or sharing it with others will help spread that feeling of joy.

PURGING RELATIONSHIPS

I remember the first time I read Jack Canfield's book *Success Principles* where he wrote about the principle that we are the average of the five people we spend the most time with. At the time, I was taking care of my two grandsons and working with severely depressed and traumatized clients and thought to myself, "My life is out of balance here." I didn't have a life coach, I wasn't doing things with friends, or meeting new people, and if I was the average of the five people I spent the most time with; I wasn't in a good place whatsoever.

What a great wake up call. We need to be around people who inspire us, who call us to grow and thrive, and who motivate us to become better versions of ourselves. We can also be that person to others, but a good ratio, as I have heard it said of the five people we spend the most time with, three people should be people that lift us up, and two can be people we help lift up. But what about the people in our lives that are a constant energy drain? The friend we can't get a word in edgewise in conversation, the needy relative that constantly stops by and takes up hours of our time, or the negative friend that we stay in touch with out of obligation because we have been friends so long.

Quantum physics tells us, when we are in close proximity to another person, we are actually exchanging subatomic particles with that person; quite literally, we are becoming a part of each other. What kind of energy do we want coming into our personal field?

Internationally renowned Japanese scientist Dr. Masaru Emoto found that the influence of our thoughts, words, and feelings on molecules of water induced profound results. Using high-speed photography, Dr. Emoto discovered that crystals formed in frozen water reacted to the concentrated thoughts that were directed to them. Water exposed to negative thoughts resulted in dull, asymmetrical patterns, often incomplete, whereas the water exposed to loving words were beautiful, brilliant, complex, and ornate snowflake patterns.

The *Journal of Biological Chemistry* 158, states that the brain and heart are mostly composed of water and that water makes up most of our muscles and kidneys. If water responds so strongly to the energy of the words and thoughts directed to it, it makes sense that being made up of so much water we would also be heavily influenced by the words we hear around us and especially the repetitive words and energy from the five people we are most in contact with.

Cultivating positive relationships, hiring a coach, joining a group that shares highest interests or goals—these are the places to put precious and vital energy. I learned that when I surrounded myself with people who were thought leaders, visionaries, and change makers, I adopted their energy and began to integrate their thoughts and ideas into my own inspired wisdom that I now share with others. As I have been lifted up in mind and spirit, my capacity to help ignite others' lives has increased ten-fold.

Purging the relationships that don't serve us opens a pathway that leads to unfolding enlightenment, self-realization, and a deep honoring of self. In therapy sessions, I have heard many clients say to me, "But I *love* him (or her)" as a reason for staying in the relationship. But love is NOT enough. We can love lots of things that no longer serve us: sugar, excessive shopping, getting high, fatty foods, and the list goes on. When it comes to loving people, I tell my clients, "The feeling of love is never wrong; however, staying with someone who is toxic, just *because* you love them, is something that will never serve you."

It has been a tremendous joy in my life to watch people heal their relationship with themselves, and to truly deepen their self-love enough to get to the point they are able to leave a toxic relationship which was binding them and sucking them dry, and to go on and flourish and expand beautifully into their own lives. When we value ourselves, we are no longer willing to compromise our well-being for a sense of comfort that may have been tied to staying with what was familiar, even if what was familiar was dragging us down. We can claim our worth and our lives when we purge the relationships that don't serve the growth and evolution of our highest selves, the selves we came into this life to fully discover and develop.

I remember talking with a client who was fearful of leaving a toxic relationship with a verbally abusive partner who would literally lock him in the closet for hours during their fights. "I guess I'm afraid of being alone and feeling lonely," he said. "I hate how I am living, but I am used to it and I don't know how to get out."

I suggested to him that while moving out and being alone

might include times of loneliness, he was already living alone in a loveless relationship that had been in a cycle of abuse for years. I encouraged him to look at what were the deeper reasons he was staying there and the costs and benefits to him and his very soul. He got the message from his deeper self. He realized that living free from fear of being verbally and sometimes physically assaulted, constantly walking on eggshells, and the potential of being literally locked inside a toxic relationship, would give him a deeper connection to himself, a sense of happiness, and deeper meaning in his life. He decided that living alone, instead of feeling alone in the hell he had been in, would be the best decision he could make for himself.

Years later, when he contacted me to let me know how he was doing, he was thriving, had taken up 10K running again, was in a fabulous relationship, and felt excited about the possibilities his future held. By purging his toxic relationship, he renewed his spirit and allowed his passion for life and love to be reignited in an expansive way.

DETACHING WITH LOVE

Five years ago, I divorced my father and stepmother.

I finally finished an email that I had been writing and rewriting for over a year, pushed send, and stepped into a whole new place in my life. I gave birth to the happiest, healthiest, most fierce version of myself I had ever known, and I reclaimed my life.

The letter had started a year before it was sent, with the help of a therapist and a deep desire to heal my life. I had spent thirty-six years trying to earn my father's love and approval. Over and over again, I had swallowed my voice, my love, and my vibrancy to just get to be around him. I felt like the underlying messages always were, "Make us proud, but don't shine too bright." "Remember you are number two. You are not special." "How you loved your dad is not allowed here and may not be expressed."

I had swallowed the beautiful relationship I had shared with my father for the first thirteen years of my life, and it had been replaced by a relationship where love was no longer unconditional. It had to be earned and what I said and did were severely judged with the ever-looming consequence of being shunned and all communications severed (which at one point lasted for three years when I was twenty-two).

Without going into all of the painful details, an example of the dynamics I experienced in that relationship came right before my brother's college graduation when I received a letter from my dad and stepmom stating, "Because you have chosen not to have a relationship with us, we will not be approaching you with signs of affection. We won't be speaking to you so don't speak to us."

After my brother's graduation ceremony, I was face to face with my parents, whom I hadn't seen in over a year, and they acted as if they didn't see me. At one point, someone asked to take a picture of my brother and wanted my dad and I to stand on either side of him. I could barely breathe. I had graduated from college the year before, and it had gone unacknowledged by them. The picture was snapped, and dad tapped me on the shoulder and said, "Hey Steph, we were proud of you too." I turned around and walked away as tears streamed down my face. He didn't speak to me again for two more years.

When I was finally writing the letter decades later with my therapist, I was ready to send it when on a random Wednesday, I received a call that my father had fallen during a walk around the lake and had suffered a major heart attack. A dentist who had been walking right behind him, saved his life by administering CPR until the paramedics could get there. They had to shock his heart back to life, and he flatlined during the process. Minutes went by. When he arrived at the hospital, because he had suffered a lack of oxygen, they put him in a hyperbaric chamber where he was "frozen," a technique that is used to slow down brain damage when someone is oxygen-deprived.

My brother and I met at the airport in Denver and flew to Austin as soon as we were able to. Dad was in a coma and was being kept alive by machines. When I walked into his hospital room a week after he had fallen, I said, "Hi, Dad," and he opened his eyes.

Everyone in the room was in tears.

My stepmother told me, "He has been calling out for you in his sleep. I knew he would wake up when he heard your voice."

It was the single most-validating sentence she had ever said to me. My father continued to come out of the coma very slowly and when awake, spoke only a few sentences in a very childlike state, but they were a soothing balm to my soul; a healing salve for the little girl who still lived within me. The three phrases he would repeat to me as I sat beside him were, "You're beautiful," "You're precious," and "I love you."

It was as if all the past and other parts of his personality had been stripped away and only the pure and loving essence of him remained. For the first time in my adult life, I knew without a doubt that my father truly loved and adored me. His essence knew mine, and it remembered that it was okay to tell me his true feelings.

After a week, I flew home. It took my father a month to have enough brain functioning for them to do the surgery. After a quadruple bypass and months of physical therapy, he finally began to physically heal. As he healed, he became more and more of the personality I had known in my later years of growing up, and less and less his essence.

The critical tone came back, the conditional love that could be retracted in a moment came back, and his joint criticism of me and my children returned. No longer were there conversations that were warm and pleasant. They were again replaced by an awkward and strained triangle that I entered into with he and my stepmother where it was always made clear, I was the odd one out.

It's hard to describe without going into a bunch of stories here, but the pain and emotional abuse I suffered for decades in this relationship was devastating. What I will share with you here is that after a harsh, critical, cold, and uncompassionate phone call from them a year later, I had finally reached my end point. It was only moments before that call, that my then-husband and I were to welcome forty people to our home for a housewarming party and I was upstairs in the bathroom crying, reeling from their harsh words that had gutted me once again. For decades, they had the ability to derail me and had once again ripped me open during this conversation, and something inside of me finally stood strong and proclaimed, "No more."

In the email I finally composed, I told them both how much I loved them. I thanked them for the gifts that each of them had given me during my life: love of music, theater, academia, and literature. I told them both how much they meant to me and how their actions at my brother's graduation, the years they had shunned me, and their twisting of my words and using them against me over and over again throughout the years had deeply wounded me.

I shared the pain of never being able to just have a healthy father-daughter relationship where I could call my dad for advice or share special moments like going to a movie or just out to lunch like we used to when I was young. I told them that I had always accepted my stepmom and how much I loved her and that my wanting to have a relationship with my father was never at the exclusion of her, even though she had told me at fifteen she considered me "the other woman." I spoke of the gifts my daughters were in the world and how deeply hurtful their severe critique of my children and me had been. And I ended the letter with, "I deeply love you both, and I don't ever want you to contact me again."

Writing the letter had taken over a year. But with that phrase, I was finally able to push the send button and never look back. I remember walking into the kitchen after I had sent the email and hugging my husband and feeling a thousand pounds lighter. My life has never been the same. Since then, I have learned to grow a closer relationship with myself. I have befriended and continued to heal the wounded parts of myself; I have thrived, my children have thrived, and my life has been extraordinary. My relationship with my mom and stepdad is just as wonderful and supportive as it has always been, even more so now with more joy, love, and energy to share.

My partner reminded me today how my healing around my father has come full circle. He said, "You speak so favorably about your dad, if no one knew what you went through, you would think your relationship with him is still like it was your first thirteen years of life."

It is true. My father had such a powerful, positive impact on my life those first thirteen years and I can still hold on to those times that were precious, meaningful, and sacred. All the wonderful memories are mine and what happened between us and how painful the relationship was the rest of my life, doesn't make any of those younger memories any less special. I had done my work throughout my life and within my heart around our relationship, so that when I was finally ready to let go, I could do so with total love and reverence for the wonderful times we did share. I could honor him and the gifts he had given me in my life and hold on to the parts that I treasured. Nothing can take that away.

Somehow, we get the message that if someone is a family member, then we must stay in relationship with that person no matter how we are treated. This could not be further from the truth. Our well-being and emotional health are essential and need to be the priority in our lives. We don't need to sacrifice our peace, happiness, or joy by staying in a toxic relationship. Life is a precious gift. How we open, express, and live that gift is up to us. We can learn how to detach with love. It doesn't have to be harsh or dramatic. We can acknowledge the gifts someone has given us (if there are any), acknowledge the relationship for what it is, and we can choose not to be in it. Most of us wouldn't stay in a relationship with a person outside of our family who was being emotionally, verbally, or physically abusive. We don't have to stay in a familial relationship that is toxic either.

For the last fifteen years, I have been absolutely devoted in my psychotherapy practice to helping mothers and daughters, fathers and sons, and all different configurations of family relationships heal. As I have said, my deepest mission is to bring as much love and healing to the world as possible. And, while I will support my clients with all of my heart, I do not support them staying in abusive or toxic relationships with ANYONE. When we truly begin to love and honor ourselves and own our self-worth, we no longer tolerate abusive relationships in our lives.

At times it takes us to the deepest and fiercest parts of ourselves to summon the courage to let go and purge these relationships that no longer serve our well-being or our lives. When we give ourselves permission to purge the abusive relationships, we ignite the healing sparks within us that eventually catch flame, and we can fiercely begin to create the boldest, most beautiful life we could ever imagine.

TAKE A MOMENT

I invite you to take an inventory of the relationships in your life. How many of them really serve you? How many increase your energy and sense of well-being and how many drain you? Learning how to say no to social obligations that are not aligned with you energetically or emotionally, or to say no to invitations to spend time with people who are negative and drain you, can be a challenge, AND it is a practice that will dramatically change your life for the better.

One of my favorite exercises from my Igniting Your Best Life group, is an exercise on purging what doesn't serve. Take a piece of paper and divide it into four columns. At the top of the page, in the first column write *Beliefs*. In the second column write *Behaviors*, in the third, *People*, and in the last, *Things*. Really allow yourself to evaluate these areas in your life one by one.

What are the beliefs you need to let go of? List the ones that are limiting you. These are the negative ones that you might say to yourself over and over again, so they *feel* true, but there isn't any evidence to support them.

Look at your daily habits and behaviors. If you press the snooze button repeatedly, overeat, or overspend, look at what behaviors need to go and what positive behaviors you could replace them with. Even if your habit is biting your nails or interrupting others, being able to look at what behaviors don't serve you and starting to work at implementing new ones are life changers. Just being conscious of when the behavior occurs and not just letting it be on automatic pilot, is the beginning of being able to change it. Saying the negative behavior out loud before you follow through, such as, "I want to eat a box of cookies." can begin to give you awareness of what was once unconscious and then you will have more of a choice if you want to follow through with that behavior or not.

Look at your relationships. Are there ones that drain you and leave you feeling emotionally sucked dry? Is there co-dependency that needs to be purged so the relationship can continue but in a healthier manner? Do you stay in relationships out of obligation but there isn't any joy? Look at where you can make a change and step into your fierce self to make these changes in your life.

Lastly, look at the things in your life that no longer serve you. Everything holds energy and if your life and your home is being clogged up with things, you aren't allowing the best energy and the highest vibration to come through. Choose to keep what brings you joy and bring joy to others by what you can share or give away. Lighten your load and breathe into the creative, flowing space it creates.

You can live an illuminated life.

You can be a conduit to allow the light, love, and highest version of yourself to come through.

This life is available to all of us. It is your time to shine.

EIGHT

THE DUALITY OF SURRENDER

*The moment of surrender
is not when life is over,
it's when it begins.*

Marianne Williamson

When we hear the word *surrender*, for many people this instantly brings up images of waving the white flag associated with the feelings of fear and cowardice. For many of us, when we have heard the word *surrender,* we connect it to a sense of giving up, giving in, and not caring. Although those definitions may surely exist in our world, to truly surrender is a brave and courageous act. When we allow ourselves to fully be in that state, it can become one of the most powerful and, ultimately, empowering acts we ever do. What manifests as a result of true surrender can be completely astounding and absolutely life changing.

I have sat across from many clients who balked at the idea of surrender. "How would it feel if you were to quit clinging to the idea that things have to be a certain way with your relationship to your daughter and just surrender to what is?" I asked one client.

"It would be a relief," he said, "but then maybe she would

feel like I was agreeing with her actions or maybe feel like I didn't care."

My client's daughter was a grown woman who chose to keep dating men that her father thought were beneath her. He told her he would never accept these "subpar" men, and this created a power struggle between the two of them and an unhealed distance in the relationship. By my client clinging to the way things "had to be" he was creating angst for both himself and the relationship.

When he was able to reframe his concept of surrender, he was able to unhook from the power dynamic. He became aware of the immense importance of having a positive relationship with his daughter and let go of trying to control her life. His anxiety and fear were greatly relieved and his daughter, not feeling so judged and rejected, became more open to working on healing their relationship. He was able to come to a place where even if he did not support her choice in men, he could still support her.

Surrender does not mean that we agree with others or their actions. It does not mean we lie down and become door mats. It means we let go of the cords that bind us emotionally to trying to control situations and other people. It means we experience more peace and freedom in our own lives.

SURRENDER AND BEING FIERCE

How can these two ways of being coexist when they seem like such opposites? Because we so often associate surrender with giving up, giving in, and being weak, how can we integrate surrender into one of the essential ingredients for becoming fierce?

Part of the duality of surrender is this: When we don't do it, we are letting outside situations and circumstances control us. When we do surrender, we take back our personal power, align with our higher selves, and connect more deeply with our trust in life. My dear friend, Jacob Liberman talks about how life will show up at the exact right time and give us precisely what we need. What would life be like if we truly believed that? We would be empowered to live life more fully in the moment because we wouldn't worry about things being any different in the present moment than they are; we would feel fearless to step into the future, knowing that life was completely supporting us and that whatever was in front of us, was perfect for the continued growth and evolution.

Surrender can have such weak connotations in our world.

It takes amazing strength and courage to say, "I am going to trust something greater than myself to handle this for me," or "I am going to accept the present moment exactly as it is, even if it is very painful." This can seem extremely counterintuitive. Our brains, which are hardwired to protect us, automatically go into fight or flight mode and our anxiety gets stirred up and it says to us, "You have to do something NOW!"

In actuality, we don't have to *do* anything. When we allow the feelings to be there, breathe through them, and accept what is happening in this moment, we are able to build resiliency. It helps to strengthen the inner muscle that says, "I can handle it when things get rough. I have made it through difficult challenges in the past, and I can do so again."

When we are pushing against how things are in this moment, it is like trying to push a large stone uphill. It doesn't make us stronger or more balanced; it causes disharmony, angst, and a sense of overwhelm or helplessness. By moving towards allowing this moment to be exactly as it is, we become better equipped to deal with life circumstances, knowing that they will constantly ebb and flow. By riding the tide of the moment, we can get to the other shore feeling more anchored in ourselves and begin to feel we have the inner-stuffing and fierceness to navigate the waters.

Michael Singer, who wrote *The Untethered Soul*, also has a great online workshop called Living from a Place of Surrender, The Untethered Soul in Action. In this fantastic and challenging course, he describes the true cause of unhappiness for most of us is that we are so focused on things going "our way" and that when they don't, we are unhappy. The opposite is true as well; when things go our way, then we can be happy. His challenge is, "What if we just accepted the present moment just as it is and didn't cling to or desire it being any other way?" "What would happen if we just surrendered to the moment?"

Believe me, I know this isn't easy. When we are in a crisis, or things are difficult, it's hard to say, "Yep. I am just going to accept this horrible thing and surrender to it being here!" It is more nuanced than that.

To better describe this, I want to share one of my learning moments with you around this. About eight years ago, my doctor found precancerous cells on my cervix. The treatment was six weeks of weekly visits to have Aldera (a cream that kills cancerous cells) applied to my cervix.

My doctor had warned me that the first couple of treatments might be easy, but that it might get more difficult as we continued and that we could take a break at any time if it became too unbearable. After those first two treatments were over, I remember thinking, *Whew! I think I may just be able to breeze through this. I feel fine!* Little did I know, the next treatment would pack such a wallop, that I was nauseous and exhausted for a week. My body ached and I felt like I had a bad flu. Just the thought of going back to the clinic for the next treatment made my stomach turn and my anxiety ramp up.

We ended up taking two weeks off. The next treatment seemed even worse. My body ached, I felt sick, and I couldn't sleep at night. I was angry that I had to go through this and was truly feeling overwhelmed trying to deal with the physical manifestations of the treatment while continuing to see a full load of psychotherapy clients. And then, one night when I was up at 3:00 a.m., on the way back from the restroom, I heard a voice in my head say, "You are making this so much harder on yourself. By constantly being angry and fighting this, you are making this so much worse!" Ah, yes. The old saying, "What we resist, persists."

I went and lay down on my bed and took some deep breaths and began to let go. I allowed all the pent-up energy of resistance to release and began to find some room within my body where comfort could come in and I could begin to relax. I fell deep into sleep, and although I still woke up feeling some nausea and discomfort the next morning, I had a deep sense of peace that followed me through the next two treatments and made all of it much more bearable. I had made peace with the present moment and that gave me an amazing amount of comfort.

Did I want to have precancerous cells on my cervix? No, of course not. But the reality was, they were there, and they were being treated, and by not fighting what was happening in my body, I could surrender to the moment and help create more healing by moving into a place of peace and no longer exacerbating the fight or flight mechanism in my brain to keep pumping more adrenaline and cortisol into my system, making it harder for me to heal. I was able to get through the rest of the treatments from a totally different place. Surrendering changed my entire experience and brought me deeper well-being along the journey.

MAKING PEACE WITH THE PRESENT MOMENT

One of the ways I work with clients and teach them how to reduce anxiety, ruminating, and fear in their lives, is to surrender to the present moment. When we give in to the media and all of its fear mongering or when we start to worry about what is going to happen in the future, we experience panic and overwhelm. None of what we are focused on in the future is actually happening, but whatever we hold in our minds, our minds experience as happening *now*. That is why we have a physiological response when worrying about the future. We start feeling anxious, thoughts race, and palms sweat. The same is true when pulling up a painful memory and the experience of regret, and heartache return. Those moments are experienced again physiologically, though none are happening in the present moment.

The good news is, the same is true with pleasant memories. When we hold something in our minds that we have a positive connection to, we begin to feel the positive emotions and pleasant body sensations as well. We start to experience a sense of well-being, as dopamine is being released in our brains. I do a safe place imagery with my clients that asks them to bring a favorite place to mind and focus all of their senses on re-experiencing that place. It is a powerful exercise that also goes beyond the five senses and asks them to move into their heart center and notice the emotions that are connected to this place, and then to find a touch point to anchor this safe place to muscle memory.

This is not an exercise to avoid a feeling or to escape reality in any way. It's a tool for moving into the present moment and out of the past and future. Daily practice (even for just two minutes) will start to carve new neural pathways that will help form the habit of feeling good and will help return more quickly from these trips into fantasy about the future or past. When we are not in the present moment, we are in fantasy. We are fantasizing about something that is not happening now. We have the power to reel ourselves in from either of these places and shift how we are feeling. And as I always tell my clients, "If you are going to fantasize about the future, you might as well make it a good one!"

BIG MOMENTS OF SURRENDER

One of my biggest moments of surrender came four years ago when I put my daughter in treatment for three months and took over the care of her three- and four-year-old sons. My daughter had struggled with addiction and alcoholism for ten years. It took everything in me to go to her home that night and confront her. I knew she had been drinking and it was time for her to surrender to her own healing journey. She didn't fight it.

She was ready. After a rough go of finding the right place for her, and finding the funds to pay for her stay, I was faced with the reality of taking care of two very scared little boys who had been through a lot. I worked full time in my private practice and the rest of my days were spent cooking, cleaning, and caring for the boys.

The first week of this was especially hard during the transition into my then-husband's and my home, and emotions ran high. My husband was out of town at a conference that first week and I was left alone to help these precious little boys integrate into a new home and a new routine that was unfamiliar to them. Those were hard days.

One night, after I had read a bedtime story to the boys, I lay my head on the nightstand in- between their beds, absolutely exhausted as I rubbed both of their backs in their little twin beds that ran parallel to each other in our guest bedroom. When they were finally asleep, I walked back to my bedroom and was struck by how alone I felt. I had gone from a happy and easy, jet setting life with my husband, to a total 180-degree change of childcare, diapers, and wild emotions. I felt so hurt, angry, confused, and overwhelmed as I thought about my daughter and the struggle she was in and how the whole family was being affected by it. I thought about the strain my marriage was under because he had refused to help me support my daughter financially because it wasn't his biological daughter and as a businessman, he had said he didn't want to invest in anything where there wasn't a guarantee for a return on his investment.

Angry, overwhelmed, and deeply, deeply sad, I literally hit my knees beside the bed and just started praying. For the first time in my life, I surrendered my life to whatever the divine's will was for me. I knew I couldn't fix anything—there was nothing I could do—and trying to push my will in life was not working whatsoever. I prayed that the divine would work in me and through me and guide my life, every element of it. Not just the convenient parts that were easy to surrender over but the entirety of my life, in all areas and in all ways.

I went to bed and slept more deeply than I had in years. I awoke feeling lighter, renewed, and aware that something had shifted inside. My life from that point on was never the same. The time with the boys was challenging and beautiful and some of the most precious memories of my life. Due to the strain in my relationship, my marriage ended, and I happily reclaimed the next chapter of my life. My daughter healed and remains in recovery, is happily married, finishing her college degree, and absolutely thriving in her life since her own surrender.

A little over a week after my surrender, I was sitting in my office thinking about how I could get into radio again, as I had been a guest of several shows and really loved it. No sooner was that thought in my head than there was a knock on my office door. When I answered, in walked a gentleman who was the friend of a friend who said he had been wanting to talk with me. He sat down, looked at me, and asked, "Have you ever thought of doing your own radio show?" Later, he would talk about how I was so excited when he asked that, that I nearly came out of my chair!

For the last four years, I have been the host of *The Spark with Stephanie James* radio show and podcast, and it has been one of the most wonderful things in my life and has opened huge worlds to me. It has been a catalyst that has led to meeting hundreds of thought leaders, wisdom keepers, and change makers in our world, producing my first film, *When Sparks Ignite*, (filmed by an award-winning film crew), and expanding my speaking and transformational coaching career in huge ways.

When I surrendered, the whole universe lined up to support me. My first book, *The Spark: Igniting Your Best Life* was published two years ago, and I have been interviewed on numerous radio shows and podcasts. Many of the people I interviewed have become some of my dearest friends and precious members of my soul family. My radio show is broadcast worldwide, and my events are international, with presenters from all over the world.

After my surrender, magical things continued to happen. I

was gifted a trip to Maui with my daughter, spent two beautiful mornings having breakfast with my now dear friend Jacob Liberman, and have traveled to exquisite and breathtaking places around the world. Two years ago, I met the love of my life, and we continue to create a beautiful and deepening relationship daily. Life has continued to blossom in ways I never could have imagined.

I continue to make surrender a part of my daily practice. In my morning meditation, I consciously surrender my entire life to the divine, and to the divine consciousness that is better able to guide my life than I am. I release EVERYTHING: my career, my abundance, my relationship, my family and friends, and my relationship with myself. By surrendering it all, I am filled with a deep peace, and a knowingness that not only does the universe have my back, but also that greater things are in store for me than I could ever imagine, hope for, or cling to. By surrendering to the divine flow of life, my soul is free. I want this kind of freedom for everyone.

TAKE A MOMENT

Take time to do an internal inventory about what you would like to surrender. It is more powerful to write these down and if you can, burn them in a fireplace (or outside in a fire pit or even in a bowl where it is safe to do so). As you watch the smoke begin to rise, imagine the energy connected to what was written down leaving your being and allow it to be completely released.

Breathe into that feeling of release and allow yourself to breathe deeply into a more expanded place inside of you. Now that you have created space, fill it with a sense of the divine or your higher self and let that energy radiate through your heart center, filling you with love, light, and peace. Focus on new and beautiful things that you would like to create, manifest, and enjoy in your life and feel into them with a knowingness that they are already on their way.

Cultivating this practice is a way to life mastery. It can become a ritual you practice on the full moon which is a time for letting go and bringing new energy into your life.

It is true. "The moment of surrender is not when life is over. It's when it begins."

NINE

WHAT'S SERENDIPITY GOT TO DO WITH IT?

It's all serendipities with no beginnings and no ends.
Such infinitesimal possibilities through which love transcends.

Ana Claudia Antunes

We are born with an inner GPS. This guidance system is hardwired into us and is one of our most trusty allies if we allow ourselves to get quiet enough to listen to it. Our intuition is always available to us and is the quiet voice that whispers in our ears (or at times has to yell to get our attention). It is the divine speaking to us at the micro level. Chills, gut feelings, a sudden knowingness that guides our decisions, are all a part of this divine program that is physiologically wired into us and is available in all moments.

If we are able to pan out from this micro place inside of us, we can expand to the bigger picture of our lives and as we look at our life as a series of roadmaps, we will start to notice the guideposts of our lives, which oftentimes have shown up as serendipity. Being in the right place at the right time might be a simple decision to talk with someone who becomes the person to later marry, or maybe deciding to delay a departure and then barely missing a fatal wreck, and many other coincidences which all become part of the intricate and divine guide helping everyone navigate through life.

Scientist, futurist and listed as, Who's Who in the World, Stephan A. Schwartz talked about this powerful serendipity in his own life when he was interviewed for my film *When Sparks Ignite*. He discussed a particular evening in the 1960s, when he was a twenty-year-old successful filmmaker at a party in Manhattan given by Truman Capote. Stephan said at one point when he was coming back from the bathroom, he passed an old gilded Italian mirror and looked at himself and said, "You have become a very unattractive person. Your values are all screwed up." He had never had that thought before.

Stephan left the party and drove to Virginia Beach and slept on the beach that night—for the first time in his life—in a state of existential depression. That night became the catalyst for a huge life transformation. He started experiencing serendipitous events after that and ended up leaving film and theater to study the works of Edgar Cayce for the next five years leading to his spiritual awakening.

Stephan went on to become a phenomenal research scientist, who was an important part of the Civil Rights movement in the '60s, military reform in the '70s, and citizen diplomacy between the United States and the Soviet Union in the '80s and '90s.

His life has been focused on exploring extraordinary human functioning, and how individuals and small groups have and can affect social change. A pioneer in consciousness research, and an internationally known researcher, his explorations on the submarine *Deep Quest* were part of a television series with Leonard Nimoy's *In Search Of.* Stephan is the author of *The Schwartz Report*, a fact-based daily publication in favor of the Earth, the interconnectedness and interdependence of all life, democracy, equality for all, liberty, and things that are life-affirming. All of this—his amazing contributions to our world, his phenomenal life of exploration—came from a single decision to leave a party. Stephan paid attention to the serendipity that showed up in his life and because of this, has made a radical difference in the lives of millions of others. What would happen if we woke up to the serendipity and signs showing up in our own lives? What might we create for ourselves and others? Just how magical might our lives be?

A Chance Meeting

When Morgan, my partner, and I are out with other couples, we are often asked how we met. It was total serendipity, and of course has changed my life forever. I had just picked up my cell phone when there was an announcement, "Friendship Suggestion," from my Facebook account. I clicked on it and saw his picture with a TEDx Talk banner in the background. Since I am always looking for new guests to be on my radio show, I clicked, "Friendship Request," and didn't think about it again. Even when I saw he had accepted my request and had sent me a message, I was too busy to open it or reply. I was in the middle of film edits, was casually dating someone else, and had a full-time private practice.

Two weeks later, when I read the message it said, "I love our mutual friends!" I had no idea who he was talking about. I clicked on his profile and saw the first mutual friend that popped up and it happened to be one of my very dear friends who was in my women's spirituality and Random Acts of Kindness group in Fort Collins, Colorado. He lived in Seattle. *No way!* I thought! *This is wild.*

When I called that friend to tell her that I had connected to Morgan she said, "Don't you remember, I told you about him a year ago! I thought you two would be perfect for each other!" I had been too busy at the time planning The Spark Summit, and organizing guests, film crews, and event platforms to even think about dating.

I reached back out to Morgan and wrote that I would love

to connect on a zoom call and to see if he would be interested in being a guest on my show to discuss his TEDx Talk. He replied, "Yes!" and that Friday we jumped on a video call. At the end of that conversation he said, "I feel like we have a lot to talk about. Do you want to jump on a call next Friday?" We did, and that conversation lasted four and a half hours, and we haven't stopped talking since. After a year of dating long distance, we moved in together and have shared the most phenomenal, spiritual, love-based relationship I could have ever imagined. He is the love of my life and truly shows up as the most incredible human being I have ever met.

His life has been a testament to following his intuition, his inner GPS, and looking at the guideposts that the serendipities in his life represent. A decade before we met, he had lived in Fort Collins for seven years. It was then when he was on a spiritual trip down to Mexico and Central America that he was briefly introduced to a woman by a mutual friend, and ninety seconds after meeting her knew he would move to Seattle to study under her as his spiritual teacher and mentor.

This move changed his life dramatically. Already a healer and chiropractor, Morgan learned deeply held spiritual traditions and ways of helping people heal at the deepest levels. As a shamanic practitioner, combined with his Certified High Performance Coaching and chiropractic work, he helps individuals heal in truly deep and holistic ways.

Together, we are aware of the way serendipity continues to show up in our lives. The right person shows up, the interview turns into a lifelong friendship, the opportunities that seem to arise out of the ethers, a chance meeting that turns into projects, and partnerships that create beautiful things in this world. We pay attention to what shows up and recognize that spirit speaks to us in many ways. When we are in alignment, serendipity is our constant companion. People, places, and things line up to help us accomplish our dreams and our goals. And we realize, we are not unique to this inner GPS made manifest in the outer world. We all have the ability to utilize the gifts of intuition, deep listening, and awareness of the signs that show up in our lives as roadmaps, guiding us forward towards an even greater expression of ourselves.

DEEP LISTENING

The more I have learned about the science of HeartMath, the more profound a tool it has become in my life. The heart has an intelligence all its own that can act as a more reliable source for us when we are asking the most important questions in our lives. The brain can get trapped in loops of logic and ego and is clouded by our past beliefs and experiences as the lens through which we view life. We can bring our heart and brain into coherence which increases order and harmony in both our psychological and physiological processes.

Our breathing patterns modulate the heart's rhythm. By breathing slowly and regularly we can generate a coherent heart rhythm. And when we breathe deeply, put a hand on our heart, and focus on a heartfelt positive emotional state, we can access our deeper knowing and intuition, creativity, cognitive enhancement, and an inner guide that we can truly rely on.

In order to notice the serendipity that appears in our lives, we have to be aware enough to notice it and open enough to receive it. HeartMath is just one of the many tools available to us to bring our hearts, brains, and bodies into fuller alliance and create greater well-being and awareness to us.

FIERCE SERENDIPITY

There are many times when life shows up to let us know we are on the wrong path as well. A decade ago, I was dating a man that my children did not like and did not want me in a relationship with. This should have been my first sign. But I ignored it. I thought they just didn't like that he was younger than me. I remember after several months of dating, I began to hear an almost audible, "No, *no*, NO!" from the universe when I inquired about if this was a right relationship for me or not.

He and I began to fight, and the fights became more intense and explosive. Then the signs from the universe got bigger. Speeding tickets, wrong orders brought to us at restaurants, a broken propeller on the boat we rented, and getting bit on the face by a spider were just a few of the signs. On and on it went until one day I said, "Enough! I get it! This is not in alignment with my higher self!" and I was done.

The day after we broke up, I was walking outside to the shed in my backyard and noticed a piece of chalk that my grandson had left on the sidewalk where he had been drawing pictures. It was in the perfect shape of a heart. *How weird!* I thought to myself. It was so striking I took a picture of it.

The next day, I noticed a rock that was embedded under the trash can when I moved it to take the trash to the curb. Again, it was in the shape of a perfect heart. I thought, *What a coincidence!* and grabbing my phone, took a picture of it as well. I soon found out this was no coincidence. Day after day, the hearts appeared in rocks, leaves, marks on the street, even in my food. As I continued to document these many hearts appearing in my life, I finally realized it truly was the universe speaking to me. It was as if the universe was giving me the direct message, "You are finally on the right track. Thanks for listening to your heart." The photo book of those hearts remains a testament of the power that serendipity plays in our lives and the importance of truly listening.

It can show up as positive or negative outer events, dreams, inner whispers, circumstances, and signs. When we become attuned to these many signs in our lives, we harness a miraculous power that can guide us in living a fierce life full of purpose and aligned with our highest selves. This power is always available to us, and we need only get quiet enough to listen.

The book in your hands is the result of a profound moment of serendipity. I was being interviewed by Karen Curry Parker for her podcast, *Quantum Revolution Podcast*, for my first book, *The Spark: Igniting Your Best Life*. Towards the end of the interview, she asked what my future plans were.

"I have been getting several pings about writing a new book," I said. I had started writing down ideas and lines at stop lights for several weeks. I knew the new book was somewhere in the universe, getting ready to come through and be written.

When we were off the air, Karen said to me, "My business partner Michelle and I have a publishing company and I want you to meet with her. I think we would like to publish your next book."

Two days later, I was on a phone call with Michelle Vandepas, and at the end of the call after sharing some of my story with her, she said, "Stephanie, you are fierce!"

I excitedly told her, "That's it! The title of this new book will be *Becoming Fierce!*" I could feel the book coming alive within me. I was elated and exuberant with the creative waves flowing through my very soul.

When I went to bed that night, I awoke a few hours later and wrote out the entire outline for the book.

Just like that.

Becoming Fierce happened serendipitously.

TAKE A MOMENT

Grab your journal and begin to make a list of things that seemed to "magically" show up in the last couple of weeks in your life. Write down things that showed up as a coincidence. Notice what appeared for you in repetition or the messages you received from multiple sources (a film, a book, or a friend) that were saying the same thing. See if you can remember any of your dreams and record them for the next two weeks and discern if there are any consistent themes in them. Become aware of serendipities that are nudging you in a certain direction. What are they saying?

As you ask these questions, relax, breathe deeply, put your hand on your heart, and wait for an answer. The universe (your higher power, source, the divine) is always supporting you. We become fierce in our own lives when we tune in and listen. New worlds lie waiting for us. Serendipity points the way.

TEN

HEALING THE GAP BETWEEN US

If we want the world to change,
the healing of culture and greater balance in nature,
it has to start inside the human soul.

Michael Meade

We currently live in a "cancel culture." Since the pandemic, it seems that a lot of people around the world are living in the fight or flight centers in their brain. Media focusing on the most catastrophic news it can drum up, has helped create a state of fear on the planet that is palpable. People are afraid to state their opinion for fear of being "canceled," ridiculed, banned, or cast out by others. Blogs, YouTube, and Facebook posts just disappear off the internet if the opinions expressed are not the ones desired by the powers that be. We see ugly examples of racism in our country and hate between political parties and between the vaccinated and unvaccinated people to extreme levels at times.

We live in a world gone mad.

In actuality, maybe it is better to say that we live in a world gone fearful.

When individuals are experiencing fight, flight, or freeze they are literally existing in primitive brain states. In the state of hyperarousal, the signals are not even reaching the prefrontal cortex of the brain where logic, rationality, and executive decision making occurs. When we are in this triggered brain and in a dysregulated state, thinking every opposition or challenge is a life-or-death situation, how do we help heal the fear that creates the chasms between us?

Thought leader, visionary, and director of a Waldorf school in Austin, Texas, Solomon Masala put it this way in my What We Need to Know Now-Living Wisdom for a Changing World event: "We need to start learning how to have difficult conversations with one another. We need to start operating in a way where we build safety with one another so real communication can occur." Solomon went on to speak about these difficult conversations we are faced with and how we can navigate through them more smoothly by soothing our brains with a few questions:

1. Will I have food today?

2. Do I have shelter and a place to live?

3. Does this person have a weapon?

There is a 99.9 percent chance that the answers to these questions will be, "Yes, yes," and "no," in that order. While this may seem simplistic to ask ourselves, we are helping our brain to see that it really is safe to be having this conversation, even if we don't agree with the other person. When we can step out of the fear, we can hold a place of empathy, understanding, and connection with one another. We can move into a place of heart cohesiveness where we can be curious about one another's perspectives instead of being threatened because we might not share the same opinions.

I have also found that feelings of calm and safety arise when we allow ourselves to drop into our hearts and out of our heads. When we breathe into our hearts, we can create a feeling of wellbeing, and this diverts our attention and energy away from perceiving the other as a threat. From this place, we can listen and engage in a more open and productive manner and real communication can occur.

My friend, filmmaker, and an extraordinary heart in this world, Tarek Mounib created a film that addresses these issues in *Free Trip to Egypt*. This film was an experiment in human kindness and empathy and the transformational power of human connection. Tarek, who is a Canadian-Egyptian entrepreneur, decided to fund an all-expense-paid trip to Egypt for seven Americans from diverse backgrounds in an attempt to combat the Islamophobia and prejudice that many Americans unfortunately feel towards Muslims. Tarek dealt with his own experience facing racism as an Egyptian Muslim child growing up in Canada and experienced firsthand what that felt like.

The Americans he found at Trump rallies were each paired with Muslim host-families in Egypt for ten days and the transformation and results in their lives were phenomenal. The awakening and heart expansion of an elderly self-proclaimed xenophobic couple, Ellen and Terry, stirs in the heart hope for humanity. To watch their experience of connecting and truly growing in love with the Muslim people with whom they stayed, was beautiful and deeply touching.

The film brings home the essential message that if we were to spend time with one another, in a curious, open-hearted capacity, we could break down the barriers and the limiting beliefs that separate us. The film also turned #pledgetolisten into a continuing movement. The pledge is simple and profound: "I pledge to listen to others who hold different opinions, views, or beliefs. I will try to understand their reasons and their perspectives and will respectfully express my own in return." What would happen in our own lives if we began to look at where we hold judgment of others and where we might have blinders on? How can we begin to open our hearts now?

In the film, *The Moses Code*, author of the *Conversations with God* series, Neale Donald Walsch shares that one of the things that changed his life was a practice he used, taken from the bible verse, "I am that I am." In the film, the power of placing a comma in that sentence becomes the pivotal point of its message. It becomes, "I am that, I am."

Using that phrase, Walsch discusses the transformative power of the new sentence as he walked down the street and encountered others. He said whether it was a person in a limousine, or a person living on the street, he would look at that person and say, "I am that, I am," and it broke down the barriers between them.

At the quantum level we are all a part of each other. What would our world be like if we could embrace that fact? If we were able to see the woundedness, the joy, the deep sorrow, and celebration of each human being we encountered, how would that crack our hearts open?

STARTING AT SCHOOL

I will never forget the woman I met at a casual encounter at my friend Sasha's home a few years ago. Although I don't remember her name, or the contours of her face, I deeply remember the story she shared with me, and I still carry it with me. As we sat in a sunny living room, sipping lemon iced tea, she shared a profound experience she had just been through, volunteering for a group called Rachel's Challenge at the local high school.

Rachel Scott was the first student to be shot and killed in the Columbine Shooting in 1999, which left thirteen people dead and twenty wounded.

Rachel's father told news reporters after the incident that at thirteen years old, Rachel had traced her hands on the back of her dresser and had written inside of them, "These hands belong to Rachel Joy Scott and someday they will touch millions of hearts." She had also written in her diary, "If one goes out of their way to show compassion, it will start a chain reaction."

Rachel's Challenge became a program about kindness, compassion, forgiveness, and connection with the intent of helping children connect with one another to reduce bullying, harassment, and violence. It has been presented in high schools and service clubs across the nation.

As we continued to sip our tea, this woman shared with me her experience of being involved with the three-day program. She shared about the small group she had worked with that involved one of the most popular kids who was a star player on the football team, and another boy who looked very meek and gaunt with dark circles under his eyes. When the group began, it was obvious the two boys were not friends. During group processes, it came out that the football player and his friends had teased the other boy and that their words had affected him in a very painful way shutting him down in his shell even further. As the groups continued to share their experiences and got to know one another, the woman commented that the two boys ended up becoming friends and formed a bond with one another.

But the powerful part of the story came in the description of what happened at the final assembly when all of the almost 1,400 students were gathered together in the auditorium. Students were invited to stand up and share what they had experienced over the last three days. The football player stood up and walked to the microphone behind the podium. The crowd cheered for him as he stood there facing them.

He said, "I want you to know that I stand here as a changed person. Most of you probably don't know Ray. He's a thin, pale kid, with dark circles under his eyes, that blends into the background. He doesn't have a lot of friends and he's not a kid that talks much, so you wouldn't notice him. Ray is a kid that my buddies and I have shoved into lockers and teased him about trying to be Goth with his pale skin and dark eyes. We definitely bullied Ray and didn't think twice about it, until I was in this group with him these last three days.

"You see, what I learned about Ray, is that the reason he has those dark circles under his eyes is that he is up a lot of nights taking care of his mother after her chemo treatments and is oftentimes holding up her hair as she pukes into the toilet. He is the only other person there to take care of her. Ray is an amazing guy with a huge heart.

"He said to me right before we came in here, 'It's been great getting to know you, but I imagine you won't be saying hi to me in the halls and it's okay.' But I am here to tell all of you, I WILL be saying hi to Ray, because Ray is my friend. I understand him now. Now I understand that we never know what is going on behind another person's eyes."

The football player then called Ray out of the crowd and over to the podium. The two boys embraced there in front of the entire student body as they stood up and cheered. A testament to the power of opening our ears, hearts, and minds to one another and the deep transformation that can occur within us and between us.

THROUGH THE EYES OF A CHILD

Think of how little children interact on a playground. They begin as total strangers, and, regardless of gender, race, or religious differences, within moments they are friends. The only prerequisite is a desire to play and a willingness to engage. What has happened to us? To that innocence? I truly believe we are born with pure hearts that have the capacity to love deeply and accept others unconditionally. It is our inherent goodness.

As a psychotherapist, I get it. We go through difficulties and traumas as part of the human experience; we experience war, racism, sexism, ageism, and a host of other negative experiences we encounter on the road of life. All of these "isms" and challenges can influence the lenses through which we see and can have us building walls of stone to protect our hearts from the hurts hurled at us. But how do we open hearts and return to love?

We are born with love and fear is what we learn. Yes, we have a fight or flight system in our brains, but we are also wired for love. We can learn to allow love to be the most prominent and guiding force in our lives. Love is what gives our lives meaning and helps melt fear away.

I have had the continued drive to heal the wounds inside of me and return to love so I can be a clearer conduit for the divine to flow through me so I may share that love more easily with the world. I have done years of therapy, attended spiritual retreats, did EMDR, had spiritual healings with a shamanic healer, attended countless seminars and personal growth workshops and events, worked with a quantum healing practitioner, and meditated for the last twenty-four years as a way to keep this flow going. It has been work, and I believe it is the only game in town. As we evolve and grow and heal, we are clearing the cobwebs and tilling the soil of our hearts to become fertile ground for self-love and love for one another to grow.

It doesn't have to be difficult. It does, however, require intention.

Like children, it must begin with a desire to engage, first with the interiors of our hearts and then with each other. I have found a powerful practice in the Buddhist forgiveness prayer as part of a morning practice, and the way we can begin the dualistic nature of healing our relationship with ourselves and others.

Buddhist Prayer of Forgiveness

If I have harmed anyone in any way
either knowingly or unknowingly
through my own confusions
I ask their forgiveness.
If anyone has harmed me in any way
either knowingly or unknowingly
through their own confusions
I forgive them.
And if there is a situation

I am not yet ready to forgive
I forgive myself for that.
For all the ways that I harm myself,
negate, doubt, belittle myself,
judge or be unkind to myself
through my own confusions
I forgive myself.

When we become fierce lovers in this world, we must take responsibility for our feelings and reactions. We must surrender the victim stance that we can hide behind unconsciously, and step into our empowered selves.

First, we must own our emotional experiences and know that no one can *make* us feel any certain way. The phrase, "You made me feel...." is not an accurate one. Yes, another's actions or words may hurt us, but we have the power to either internalize their behavior, or we can choose to see their behavior as a reflection of what is going on with *them* and that we do not have to take their words, energy, or behavior as our own truth.

Next, we can choose to hold on to ourselves no matter what someone else says or does. It is a hurting soul that hurts others. When we see the wound within the other, it doesn't excuse their negative behavior, it just makes room in our own hearts for compassion and empathy to occur.

In *The Four Agreements,* Don Miguel Ruiz reminds us to take nothing personally. Each person is in their own drama, their own experience of the world. I remind clients daily to remember that each person is looking at the world through their own lens that is colored by all of their own past experiences and beliefs. We don't all look at the world through the same lens. What is beautiful though, is that we can connect to each other from the deeper parts of ourselves through a universal heart if we are willing to move from our outer experience that divides us, to an inner experience that unites us.

THE SCHOOL OF LOVE

Our inherent nature as children is one of unconditional love and unlimited potentiality.

What would happen if our school systems nurtured the very best in us and recognized our inherent gifts and talents, our uniqueness, and cultivated the passions that are fierce within us? How would we be more connected to our inner selves, the world, and to each other?

I have had the profound pleasure of having the person who has been the director of the independent Upland Hills School for over forty years, Phillip Moore, on my show and in my events several times. From him, I have learned a model of how we can nurture the very best in our children and help bridge the gap between us. His book *The Future of Children* grew out of over four decades of direct experience with children who have been educated in a school that was based on love.

The students from Upland Hills School have grown up to be extraordinary people. The school nurtured a direct connection to nature and to our planet and influenced them to feel a deep connection with life. The school environment cultivated their own inner genius and taught them they could excel in their passions and live through their hearts.

What would happen if our schools were modeled after this and growing conscious, connected, and centered human beings became a priority in our world? How would this change things?

It is essential for us to begin implementing these kinds of programs that will promote creativity, connection, and higher consciousness now. Think about how lives may have been different, if what was most alive, most fierce within, was nurtured and encouraged to grow and flourish. What would that illuminated person have created in this world? What would happen if we started to allow and encourage ourselves and others to access those sparks within (that still exist) right now? How could we nurture those parts and allow them to ignite?

When we are taught that our inherent selves matter, and our

true skills, creativity, and inner genius are valued, seen, and heard, we show up differently in the world. We relate to one another from a totally different place, and we can hold each other's differences in a way where individuality is valued, and diversity is something to be celebrated because everyone's unique contribution adds strength to the collective whole.

Even if this was not our orientation in the world, we can recapture and return ourselves to our own School of Love and begin to melt our own hearts. We can take our own inventory of what is essential to us, what truly lights us up, where we need to grow and expand, and begin to educate ourselves to become expanded, creative, connected versions of ourselves. We can move into connective conversations with others where we can learn and be expanded by one another regardless of our race, religion, or backgrounds. We can learn to live fiercely through our hearts regardless of outer conditions or situations. We can make the choice that, "Today, I will live in love. Today, I choose love."

MOVING FORWARD, MOVING TOGETHER

There is no one "secret sauce" for how to bring our hearts into alignment with one another, only pointers and practices to help us get there. We have had amazing examples over the course of history. Buddha, Gandhi, Mother Teresa, Jesus, and Muhamad have shown us how to exist from within our hearts and to love others unconditionally. Their messages have inspired many other wisdom keepers in our modern world such as Deepak Chopra, Pema Chödrön, Mark Nepo, and Eckhart Tolle who have shed light on how we can heal and truly be a beacon of love to others. There is a universal thread of wisdom and an underlying current of "the truth that will set us free" running through all of their messages.

In my own decades of research, working directly with the human condition through hundreds of individuals, couples, and families as they continued their healing journey, I have found that the things that truly heal us and the love that binds us together can be deeply enhanced in the following ways:

1. Connect with yourself first (and then connect with others). Daily. We've talked about putting yourself as a priority in your own life. This is essential. Get up in the morning and practice mirror work by gazing into your own eyes and taking a moment to say, "I love you, I am here for you, I've got your back and I will take care of you." Notice the beauty that is your true essence coming through you. Notice the love in your heart and see it shining through your eyes. As you open your heart to love yourself more, you allow more love to flow to others. Think of this as an infinity sign of love flowing to you and from you and then back again.

2. Prime your mind (and your heart). Think of a memory that brings you absolute joy. Bring to mind a loved one and recall looking into their eyes. Feel the love between the two of you. See them smiling and happy and feel how that connects you even more deeply to that feeling. Breathe it into your heart space and feel it radiating like the sun. Bring all of your attention to your heart center and friction breathe into your heart space and allow the energy to expand.

   Then build on that visualization. After you have brought to mind someone you love and feel that love radiating out to them, then imagine love expanding to close friends or family. Next, allow that love to grow and emanate to acquaintances and the people you might see at the coffee shop or grocery store. Imagine that love expanding even more and reaching your entire community, then your state, your nation, and then spreading all the way around the world to all of life and all sentient beings. End with having all of that immense love come back to you to land in the center of your heart and allow it to radiate throughout your entire being. Let yourself marinate on these feelings.

3. Take responsibility for your own growth. Get out of any blame game (that includes blaming yourself for anything in your past). You have the power to choose what you want to focus on IN THIS MOMENT! Start with your daily intention of what you want to do to help yourself grow. Be mindful about what you listen to, read, and learn today. Even listening to a ten-minute video about something you want to grow awareness in will help you feel you are moving forward. If you are stuck, reach out. Call a friend or loved one, or connect with a therapist, coach, or healer that can help you resolve and re-love whatever is blocking you from flow.

   Take inventory of any energetic or mental blocks that need to be cleared for you to feel like an open conduit for love, compassion, and joy. What needs to be resolved? Forgiven? You can practice cord cuttings (cutting the energetic cords) from people you have been in conflict with to further let go of the past. Do a soul retrieval or some inner-child work to help release the bonds to the past. This gives the wounded part of yourself a voice and allows your more adult-self to hold and nurture that wounded part, allowing it to integrate more fully and to heal.

4. Think of one person who would benefit from your reaching out today and the reason it would matter to them (and you), then do it! A text, a note, a phone or video call… reaching out beyond the gap increases well-being for us and for the person who receives it.

   Marty Seligman, psychologist and research professor at Penn State, has reported that through his research, he has found the biggest "joy booster" you can have, is to write a letter of deep appreciation and gratitude to someone who has profoundly and positively influenced your life, and if possible, go read it to them in person.

The results for both of you are powerful and long-lasting.

5. Actively listen to the people you are in contact with during the day. This requires being present and dropping out of your head and into your heart. Take deep breaths to ground yourself as you move into conversations with others. Check your ego at the door and remind yourself that you are having a conversation with this person for the purpose of understanding and connection, not to determine who is right or wrong.

6. Spend one minute a day visualizing your partner and seeing them at their best. Remember a time that you laughed together or experienced a moment of deep connection. Because our minds do not have a sense of time, you will experience all of the positive chemical reactions emotionally and physiologically in the present moment as if it were happening now.

   Take this one step deeper. Spend one minute today visualizing someone you may be having a conflict with, or that you have unresolved issues with, and imagine them as an innocent, wounded child. See that person as an adult with the wounded little child still alive inside of them and send light, love, and healing to that wounded part of them. You will be amazed at how the energy and dynamic between the two of you can actually shift in both of you as you continue this daily practice.

7. Educate yourself. Expand your heart (and your mind) through reading books or watching movies and documentaries about other cultures and other people's experiences throughout time. Understanding more about The Holocaust, the Civil Rights Movement, the genocide of Africans in the Congo, or about one person's account of surviving war or extreme hardship, can help begin to open our hearts and cultivate a deep sense of compassion and empathy for others.

Some great recommendations are Viktor Frankl's book, *Man's Search for Meaning*, about finding meaning despite being in a prison at Auschwitz, or the Ram Dass documentary, *Going Home*, where you witness the journey in the last part of his life after his stroke and the wisdom he shares about surrendering to what is. Pippa Scott's *King Leopold's Ghost* is about the genocide in the African Congo for the rubber trade, and David Gutterson's *Snow Falling on Cedars*, which although fiction, draws heavily from actual events following World War II and the Japanese internment camps in the Washington state area. These are all excellent sources that allow your mind to open and your heart to expand.

Of course, there are countless other resources. Understanding more about quantum physics and the fields of pure potentiality: work by Amit Goswami, Joe Dispenza, Bruce Lipton, and Natalie Ledwell, all share how we can break through old paradigms and ways of living, and experience whole new worlds inside of us and learn to manifest them in our outer world. Two of my personal favorites, Larry Dossey and Jacob Liberman, in their amazing contributions, offer us pointers to our unlimited connection to the Source, our oneness with all that is, and a roadmap of how to better navigate our lives.

As something is opened to you, allow yourself to follow the golden threads that lead you to the next source that feeds your soul. It is a beautiful unfolding and one that will weave a beautiful tapestry of deeper connection, love, and understanding in your life.

8. Touch nature. Even if it is just a walk into your backyard. Give thanks for this beautiful world that supports our very lives. Put your feet on the earth, touch a tree and stare into its branches, feel the life force that is surrounding you through all living things. Listen to the

birds and to the sweet whispering of the wind. If you listen closely enough, you may hear the whispers of your very own soul as it reverberates with all that is, in communion. Study after study shows that spending time in nature is linked to cognitive benefits and improvements in mood, mental health, and emotional well-being. Whenever possible, extend your stay. Hike, camp, go to the park. Spend time in nature leaving all of technology behind. Gaze at the stars and remember you are part of all that is in this vast and expanding universe. We are inner connected beings.

9. Spend time together. We are creatures of connection, and we need one another. Even if it just ends up that we are connecting on the internet by video, make connection time a priority in your life. Expand your circle to spend time with people from different cultures and of all different ages. We all have something to learn from one another. Think of it as a school for the soul. Our daily lessons are given through those we encounter that may offer a different way of thinking, a different perspective, and open us up to whole new worlds.

10. Practice the "I am that, I am" exercise described by Neale Donald Walsch with everyone you encounter today. Practice putting yourself behind their eyes for a moment. Here is where empathy grows and compassion flows. Challenge yourself to listen to people who have different opinions than yours and keep this, "I am that" mindset going. You don't have to agree with anyone in order to feel a sense of compassion and connection with them in their humanness. At our core, we are all looking for the same things. We want to find a life of meaning and purpose for our lives. We want to be loved, listened to, and seen.

We can create a better world by doing the work internally, healing ourselves. We give rise to the ocean of healing that can help heal humanity and this planet. There has never been a more important time than now to do this essential work. We live in a world that is often unpredictable and chaotic. By doing these practices and expanding our hearts and minds, we begin the essential work that can result in a substantial change on the planet. It begins with us. It begins with you.

TAKE A MOMENT

Think of one way, from the above list, that you are willing to try out today and commit to doing it. You get to choose how you show up today and you are a powerful creator in your own life. Expand your sense of self, reach out to others, and begin to build that beautiful bridge that will truly help heal the gap.

ELEVEN

IGNITING THE FLAME

When the fire of your soul ignites the passion within your heart,
don't view it as an opportunity for success or failure,
view it as an open door for miracles.

Jennifer Finney Boylan

Our life experience can often define us. We must break out of the preconditioned version of ourselves so we can start creating a new story—one where we are the main character and we live fully lit up, confident, connected, contributing, and in community with others. It starts with a daily practice of intention, attention, and commitment to being awake, alert, and grounded in the present moment. Utilizing the supports around can help to live in fierceness more fully.

I worked for four months with transformation coach Ken Foster, a visionary, business strategist, and bestselling author. He challenged me to stretch my version of myself, act with courage, and put myself out into the world in expanded ways. In his life, he overcame a dysfunctional childhood, grew up with multiple failures, and started his career as a gas station attendant, but later went on to run a $200 million dollar a year securities business. At the top of his career, he had a fall from grace and a dark night of the soul which transformed his life and his career. From that, he found the inner gifts of courage, passion, wisdom, and grace, and he has created an unbelievably fulfilling and successful life.

Currently, at over sixty years old, he is a triathlete who was on team USA in 2017 and competed in the ITU World Triathlon Championship placing top ten in the world in AquaBike. An internationally sought keynote speaker, Ken has shared the stage with Jack Canfield, Steven R. Covey, Bob Proctor, Marci Shimoff, Les Brown, and Mark Victor Hansen among countless others.

We cannot grow in the dark. An essential piece in my relationship in working with the coaches I have, is that they have helped me see aspects of myself that I was unable to see alone. We need mentors, coaches, and partners that can help us capture what is fierce within us and help us to ignite our inner flame.

While we can do major transformational work alone and gain wisdom and knowledge within us, at the same time, it is invaluable to have other people shining their light of insight, wisdom, and experience on us. Other people can reflect to us the gifts, value, and magic they see sparkling within us that we may not be able to see within ourselves because our lens is clouded with our own subconscious limiting beliefs and experiences. They also might see places where we are stuck and need to grow that we are not even aware of.

I have had many clients over the years say a version of, "I felt like I was doing great alone and now that I am in a relationship, all of my stuff is getting triggered!" We can look great alone. It is only when we are in a relationship that the unhealed parts of us are more clearly revealed and can be mirrored to us by another. This can be a deep friendship or a life partner. The closer we are, the safer we feel, the more our unhealed parts rise to the surface. One of my favorite sayings around this is, "Love brings up anything *unlike* itself for the purpose of being healed." Our relationships are the balm that can help heal our souls and ignite new worlds within us.

If we want to be fierce and feel fully ignited, we need others' reflections of our flame. Through these reflections, we are better able to burn away what doesn't serve us, let go of old dysfunctional thought and behavior patterns, and expand our best version of ourselves.

Match Points

There are so many contributors to what ignited the flames within me. At nineteen years old, I began my dive into the realms of consciousness, connection, and expanded ways of experiencing what was lit up inside of me. I attended workshops in Denver on Transfiguration with Leonard Orr and Rebirthing seminars with Sandra Ray. I began reading everything I could get my hands on to help explain how we can truly connect with our higher selves, one another, and transcend our circumstances to stand more strongly together as a collective. Books on spirituality, philosophy, psychology, and science all became ingredients in this alchemical mix of wisdom and ways to live a highly conscious, connected, and cohesive life with one another.

During this time, I remember the profound moment I had while reading Leo Buscalia's book, *Love*, while soaking in a tub and deeply getting that love, as the Beatles succinctly put it, is really all there is. But how do we live more fully and fiercely from this place within us?

A profound moment for me in understanding this flame came from experiencing the loss of my forty-six-year-old Aunt Gwen who died of breast cancer. A dancer and movement therapist, Gwen was a fierce lover of life and was such a huge spark and influence in my family. She brought her native American drum to our Thanksgivings and while the thirty of us were circled up to say grace, she would lead us singing, "Now I walk in beauty, beauty is before me, beauty is behind me, above and below me," while we gave thanks to the four directions. She brought house blessings and Sufi traditions into our lives and expanded our family's experience in beautiful ways. Gwen had a laugh that filled the room and a spirit that both permeated and penetrated a concert hall. She radiated joy, deep grace, and a way of moving through the world fully empowered and unashamed.

When she received the terminal diagnosis of her cancer, I went out to coffee with her at one of our favorite coffee houses, Starry Night. As we spoke, I had the sudden realization strike my core, that she was actually going to die and that the beautiful woman I was talking to and loved and treasured, would, in a very short time, cease to exist. At one point during our conversation, I reached across the table, grabbed onto both of her arms and held them, and said to her, "Do you really want to die?" somehow hoping it was some kind of a choice and she could reverse it by just deciding that was no longer the path she wanted to take.

I carried a belief that people didn't just die unless some part of them had chosen to do so. As naive as that may sound, I couldn't wrap my mind around the fact that this vibrant, funny, effusive woman who was such a huge part of my world, would one day cease to exist.

"No," she said. "Of course not, but this is what is here now. I am going to die."

The stunning reality of her impending death pierced through me and opened my heart with a huge realization of how very, very precious this life is. This breath. This moment. Knowing her life was ending made me want to live more fully, to embrace this gift and live it more fiercely for both of us. I decided to laugh more fully, love more intensely, and deepen my exploration of what makes life more meaningful and truly lights up my soul and others.

Perhaps one of the biggest match sticks in my life has been the cultivation of my relationship with the divine. Call it Source, God, Higher Power, Allah, or any other number of names, but the awareness of that spark within us and greater than us, has continued to fortify me, ignite my soul, and make me a fierce human in this world. It is something I feel burning in me and I recognize in others. It is what I truly believe has the power to transcend our circumstances and help us heal our lives and this planet.

I remember an Easter sunrise service at Horsetooth Reservoir shortly after my grandmother died. At thirteen years old, I could sense her in the sunrise. I felt deeply connected to her loving and compassionate heart and was aware that although she was gone from this physical plane, her flame of love was still lit. She lived inside of me, and I knew our connection was timeless. The divine was in the whispers of the wind and the calling from the birds in the trees. I could see the divine in it all and it fortified me.

I feel this force in nature every time I am a part of it. I have hiked fourteeners, walked through rivers, explored caves, kayaked in bioluminescent bays, and scuba dove in oceans. In these moments I am fully alive. In these moments, I remember that the same energy that is beating through all of it, beats within me and within each one of us.

Throughout my life, this is a connection I have come home to again and again. It is always waiting as close as my breath, and is always available in me, as me. I am part of this divine flame, and it is a part of everyone too. When we tap into the divine, we become connected to all that is; we can sense our oneness with all things, and each time we return to this awareness, it is like adding lighter fluid to our inner flame. It keeps burning more intensely and becomes brighter.

This is why I think our own healing is so essential.

As we heal and start to see the divine within us, we begin to recognize it in others.

Future Lights

In his recent book, *Recapture the Rapture,* Jamie Wheal shines an amazing light on how we can create more of a collective heaven on earth as we work on healing ourselves which positively affects our communities, our collective consciousness, and our entire humanity. Through my interview with him and through his writings I have learned so much that has continued to open up worlds within me.

Jamie teaches us, through his decades of extensive research, how we can "Wake up, grow up, and show up" to create a better world for us all. He discusses the most effective protocols for healing humans in breath work, body work, substances, sex, music, and what he calls "hedonistic engineering," as ways we can expand our perspectives, process our pain, and connect with each other to manage the road ahead.

So much of his book is on finding and creating meaning in our lives and with each other, and it gives amazing research findings on the best ways for us to heal ourselves, our relationship with the planet, and each other. In his ten suggestions, that are much like the ten commandments of how to live our best life, he talks about the obvious: sleep deeply, eat real food, breathe deeply, make love, give thanks, grieve deeply, get outside, bathe often, don't do stupid shit, and know that there is no capital 'T' in truth." What we know to be true is continually changing and evolving, so what we hold as truth is not the ultimate truth, nor should we hold it over one another's head as such.

The list ended with one of the most powerful suggestions, "Above all, be kind."

What happens when we are truly kind to ourselves and one another? There is so much potential for big changes in this world. Jamie's collective wisdom in this book is an inspired view through the looking glass where what we see reflected to us, is a world where we can transcend our differences and live from a place of possibility and potentiality as we create a better world together.

As we look to other luminaries to light the way for us, we can assess what resonates within us and what becomes a part of our own inner light. In October of 2021, I put on an international event, What We Need to Know Now: Living

Wisdom for a Changing World. It brought together twenty-two thought leaders, change makers, and wisdom keepers from around the globe for the purpose of sharing what each person felt was the essential message needed in our world now. The four-and-a-half-hour event was stunning. Mark Nepo, Jacob Liberman, Tom Cronin, Natalie Ledwell, Misa Hopkins, and Amit Goswami, along with the other presenters, were the lighter fluid and the matchsticks that ignited a guiding flame that can help us cultivate resilience, courage, calm, clarity, and a way to move forward in challenging times.

Recapturing joy, telling our stories, learning how to meditate and break through limiting beliefs, learning how to wake up, grow up, and show up are all parts of the beautiful tapestry that is woven together by these amazing souls to create this one-of-a-kind, deeply supportive, and healing event. We all need guides as reminders to what we already know is true inside of us; we may have dampened the flame through trials or difficulties we have faced. But that light is always burning inside of us, even in the darkest of nights. There are times we just need others to add a little oxygen to that flame so it can once again illuminate our lives.

IGNITING WITHIN

Throughout this book, we have discussed how essential it is to cultivate a loving relationship with ourselves. It becomes even more imperative that we tend to this flame of love within us as we age. Just like we must tend to our outer relationships so they can grow and thrive, the same is true for tending this flame inside of us, towards ourselves.

There are so many messages in our world about our worth connected to what we look like and to having a youthful appearance. While this is also true for men, the message has historically been more profoundly true for women. In 2020, the American Society of Plastic Surgeons revealed that more than $16.7 billion dollars was spent on cosmetic plastic surgery and other minimally invasive procedures. What are we so desperately trying to cling to? How have we bought into an expiration date that signifies our worth is somehow inherently connected to our age?

When I was growing up, it used to be if you were a female actress past forty, your career as a leading lady was considered over. Your beauty had expired. In 2003, Diane Keaton at fifty-seven years old, broke the Hollywood standards and was nominated for an Academy Award for her leading romantic role as an empowered older woman who wins the heart of a young Keanu Reeves and the youthful, skirt-chasing attention of Jack Nicholson in, *Something's Gotta Give*. She portrayed a very successful woman, fully empowered in her career, friendships, and lifestyle. She had it all outside of having an intimate relationship. Jack, who at the beginning of the movie is actually dating her daughter, later in the film forms a friendship with Diane and despite her age, sees her true beauty and depth and falls in love with her.

This film portrayed the stereotypical male, who at first was unable to see the worth of a woman beyond her youth and looks and the importance of seeing the true beauty in someone which then created a deep and meaningful relationship. It heightened my awareness of how we as women need to embrace our own unique beauty and not see ourselves through this stereotypical lens we have adopted from our media culture of the "approved" definition of beauty. Our beauty runs deep. It is our incredible capacity to love that emanates from us that is our true beauty. We are gorgeous flames in this world and as we see our own inherent worth and value, we fall in love with the beauty of our own souls. When we grow in this depth of knowingness and love for ourselves, we will transcend this stereotype and change this "youthful curse" on ourselves, our daughters, and granddaughters.

Interestingly, I had a powerful dream last night where I was walking on a dock surrounded by water, with a beautiful, radiant, 300-pound Black woman. At one point, as we were walking, she just sort of dove sideways into the water. She was laughing heartily with an effervescent joy that surrounded her and radiated from her. In that moment, as I was looking at her, I finally got it.

She saw her beauty; she embraced it.

It was not defined by any cultural or societal norms. She *owned* her radiance. She knew she was a gorgeous force in this world to be reckoned with. The next thing I knew, I was floating through this body of water on my back on a cushioned floating pad. As I was lying there, I could feel her profound and powerful message begin to assimilate into my very being. I could feel the change taking place within me at a cellular level. As I embraced my own unique beauty that was incomparable because it was uniquely mine, I experienced an empowerment that I had never experienced before. It flowed through my veins and illuminated my entire being. This woman had infused me with a precious and transformative gift, and I knew, now that I was aware of my own beauty, that no one else could dictate nor take it away from me. I had an inner strength that was, from that dream forward, unstoppable.

AGELESS ILLUMINATION

Coming to terms with aging and embracing our inherent value is not just a female issue by any means. I have spoken with many men who have shared that there was a certain time in their lives when they felt as if they became invisible to the potential partners they were interested in. How we mentally and emotionally hold our feelings about ourselves and aging affects us all, regardless of gender or sexual orientation.

My dear friends, award winning television, film producers, and authors, George and Sedena Cappannelli, have forged a new blueprint on aging with their *Ageless Living* TV series on PBS. With an amazing cast of *New York Times* bestselling authors and luminaries in the fields of consciousness and personal development, this powerful series includes Bruce

Lipton, Gregg Braden, Thomas Moore, Anita Moorjani, John Gray, David Suzuki, and Joan Borysenco, among others and teaches us how to fiercely and beautifully thrive at any age.

From knowing and working with George and Sedena, I know how they live what they share, and they have helped thousands of others to transcend old narratives and embrace the second half of life as a time of thriving, full of meaning and purpose.

We have an opportunity to rewrite how we have mistreated and devalued the elderly and aging in America. We have beautiful examples in other countries of how the elderly are respected, revered, and honored. We can learn from these examples by studying other cultures and learning how we can begin to emulate this within ourselves and towards others. As we deepen our respect for ourselves and our own journey, we can more easily see this inherent worth in others.

There is deep wisdom in the years we have walked on this Earth and the experiences that have shaped and influenced our lives. We can look at the different decades of our lives and what was meaningful, the struggles and the triumphs, and the golden threads through it all. As we examine our lives we will begin to notice the things that guided the journey and the wisdom gained through this miraculous experience of being alive on this planet at this time.

By valuing each journey, we may find the essential messages to share with others. My hope is that all of us will also become aware that each human being on this Earth has gone through their own journeys, encountering pain, heartache, joys, and magical moments. There is power in sharing our stories and in listening to the stories of others. Perhaps through this sharing of our collective stories, we begin to weave a beautiful tapestry to hold humanity in a new paradigm of what it means to value ourselves and each other throughout our lives.

Each of us has something beautiful to contribute, regardless of our age or our point on the road map of our lives. We can claim in this moment, "I am making a commitment to live fiercely. I will fiercely love myself, others, and all life." As we are willing to open our hearts, our lives will change. Situations and circumstances around us will change. As we value ourselves, we will begin to deeply value the FULL journey we each, and others, are on as we walk, and sometimes stumble down this astonishing road we all share.

TAKE A MOMENT

How do you begin to claim a more positive version of your life? To start with, you can begin to break your old limiting beliefs by transplanting new ones. Look into your own eyes in the mirror and say out loud, "I am a powerful being of light. I have all that I need, to be all that I am. I am fierce, inherently beautiful, and loving."

Use this as a mantra. Say it (or the words your heart most needs to hear) out loud three times, whisper it three times, and then bring it into your heart and say it internally until you feel yourself begin to embrace it; until it starts to feel like it is becoming assimilated into the very cells of your body. Mark it on the calendar and do this for thirty days and watch your inner and outer world transform. As we believe, we will see this also reflected in our outer world.

This is your time to shine, to ignite the flame within, and allow it to illuminate your entire being and beyond. Imagine a tiny spark of love igniting within your soul. Gather kindling through focusing on people, places, and things that you love and begin to bring this flame to your heart. Do friction breathing into your heart space and imagine the oxygen you are breathing in, further fueling the flame. Feel the warmth and how it expands throughout your chest and beyond the boundaries of your body. Feel your flame fully ignited and its radiance expanding in all directions. Step into your day, a fully ignited human being, ready to live and love from this alive and fierce place inside of you.

TWELVE

Becoming Fierce

And one day she discovered
that She was fierce,
And strong,
And full of
fire,
And that not even She
Could hold herself back
Because her passion burned brighter
than her fears.

Mark Antony

As with all journeys, this is not the end, but only the beginning of the next adventure on your unique and beautiful path. Take inventory of what has spoken to you in this book and define what your first steps are going to be as you integrate what resonates. You have the capacity to change and the power to transform your life. Everything you could possibly want is waiting for you.

You can begin by greeting each moment with excitement, rather than control, and by breathing into the unlimited potentiality that is here for each one of us in every breath. Difficult times and challenging circumstances will continue to happen, but now you have the tools to grow grit and increase resilience, and you also have a roadmap to cultivate courage and ignite the flames of fierceness within you.

And like any flame, it must be tended or it will be extinguished. Repeating affirmations, practicing behavioral changes, and forming new habits that feed your soul will keep that flame alive within and keep you moving towards newer and better versions of yourself your entire life.

We all want meaning and purpose in our lives. You are the meaning-maker in yours! You get to define your purpose and when you align it with the deeper callings of your heart, you become unstoppable. Each one of us has the capacity to do this. What have you been waiting for? Our happiness and well-being are not outside of us, they dwell within us, with this breath. Put your hand on your heart and breathe into this moment. Feel the warmth and radiance of your own heart. It is uniquely beating JUST FOR YOU.

Your life is precious.

Let it be a celebration of the beautiful essence you came into this world with, already intact inside of you. It is never lost, only covered up at times. Unveil it. Do the excavation work to allow the sparks within you to ignite this amazing flame that is so desperately needed in our world today.

You. Matter.

Each one of us is responsible for our own healing. As we do this essential work, we become the conduits for more love, passion, creativity, health, and healing to flow into the world. Let each one of us respond to the calling of our hearts to live fully, love deeply, embrace the beauty of this moment, present our essential selves, and thrive radiantly. We have the power to break through old paradigms that keep us locked into the "not good enough" syndrome. What would happen if we just stopped believing that? What if every time that came up, we just said, "Old script, rewrite!" and affirmed our deeper truth instead? What if we really did allow ourselves to become the rockstars of our own lives? What would happen then?

We live in an abundant universe. There is enough joy, love, bliss, and compassion to go around. When we release our scarcity mindset, we see that we are enough and that there IS enough to go around because it all starts within ourselves. We are the generators. We are the dream makers manifesting our inner and outer experiences. This is not to say that life will be easy and that we will all just be floating on happy clouds eating bonbons. We live in a dynamic and interactive world that, at a quantum level, is all energy. Become a clear conduit for the energy you want to contribute to the world.

Stephan A. Swartz talked in my film, *When Sparks Ignite*, about the power we truly have as individuals to make collective change. When groups of people share a common intention, that collective intention brings about social change. When 10 percent of any given cohort, whether it is a group, a school, a community, or nation, changed, the whole cohort had to adjust. Your contribution to this 10 percent matters!

This is how social change is created and you have the power to start making change now. Make conscious choices about everyday things like the cars you drive, the toothpaste you buy, what you eat, and other everyday selections. If those decisions are based on the highest well-being for all, you can be a part of that change you want to see in the world. In the film, Stephan poses these essential questions to us: "If not now, when? And if not you, then who?" This is a powerful charge for us to begin to ignite the sparks within us and create our collective flame.

What if we just lived fiercely despite it all? What if we embraced the pain and the discomfort and let it burn inside of us until all that remained were embers, and then just smoke that eventually blew through our bodies and away? It is not ignoring the pain in our lives but experiencing it full on that empowers us. When we allow what is there to be witnessed, felt, and then released, it is transmuted, and we heal.

When we embrace the pain of others with a compassionate

heart, we become the healing balm and the alchemists in our world. Listening to Gregg Braden's book, *The Science of Self-Empowerment,* he shared about meeting with yogis and spiritual masters from all over the globe, and the most important sacred secret they shared with him about the meaning of life, came down to one word: compassion. Let us have the courage to meet this day with compassion for ourselves and for others. Let us make acts of compassion our daily practice and live fiercely with fully open and compassionate hearts. The earth, the sky, the animals, the plants, and each one of us needs this compassion. You have this power within you. You were born with it. You were born to be a contributor and in your most natural embodied self, you are this fierce compassionate heart.

I recently interviewed dynamic international public speaker, Martin Rutte about his book, *Project Heaven on Earth.* Our interview was thought-provoking and inspirational. Martin discussed the three essential questions we all need to ask ourselves as we look for a new way forward and a rewrite of our current story.

Ask yourself these three questions:

Recall a time when you experienced heaven on Earth. What was happening?

Imagine that you have a magic wand and with it you can create heaven on Earth. What is heaven on earth for you?

What simple, easy, concrete step(s) will you take in the next twenty-four hours to make heaven on Earth real?

These three simple questions can create profound and powerful results and will define a way forward for you and for others. During our interview, Martin spoke about how one person's answer to question number three was to smile at two people each day, with the concept that people will pass it on. It was mind blowing to think that if just one person did that, and then those two people each smiled at two people, in thirty-two days, the entire population of the world would have shared a smile. That's huge! If we first start with creating heaven on

Earth within ourselves, by doing our own work and cleaning out whatever cobwebs we need to get rid of in order to be a clearer conduit for our own divine spark to shine, just think how we can begin to shine that light on others and help make a significant change in the world.

I believe as we envision the kind of world we want to live in, we will begin to create and co- create it with others and with the divine. I used to believe that the only time in my life I was co-creating with the divine was the two times I was pregnant with my daughters. My phrase I would share with others was, "This is such a special time because I now have an opportunity to co-create with God." Now I know this reality of co-creation is available to us in every moment. It is the divine flowing to us, as us, and from this place we can visualize, and bring to fruition the birth of a world of harmony, peace, and interconnectedness like never before.

This is my deepest prayer for you:

May you breathe deeply into the contents of your very soul and know the vast sky of potentiality that is always available to you.

May you feel your connection to all living things through you, as you.

May you breathe deeply of the wonder and the beauty you are and acknowledge the many, many gifts that you bring to this life.

May you feel the passion, the promise, and the unlimited potential that is your true essence and allow your inner flame to burn so brightly that its warmth will be extended to all you encounter.

May you know the deepest peace in your heart, your inherent goodness, and embrace your deep sense of worth.

May you befriend the joy, the anger, and the sorrow that shows up at your doorstep and embrace them all as you deepen your love affair with your most authentic self.

You. Are. A blessing.

You truly have everything you need to become fierce in your own life. You hold the torch and have the matches that will ignite this flame. This is the essential time, and you are an essential being.

Let's illuminate this world together.

ACKNOWLEDGMENTS

It is difficult to know where to begin, as I feel such deep gratitude for the many, many people that have been fierce role models, and for those that have shown up and given me tremendous love and support throughout my life.

My first thank you goes to my amazing book coach and soul sister Shauna Hardy for her love, enthusiasm, spontaneous zoom dance parties, and for her tremendous belief in this book. I love you with my whole heart!

To my parents, Forrest and Judy Boggs for their unconditional and fierce love of our family and one another. You are my anchors.

To my beautiful daughters Acacia and Hailey, may you continue to experience the beautiful unfolding of your journeys. You have both been two of my greatest teachers and having you as my daughters has been two of the greatest gifts in my life. You are both fierce women who move through this world in amazing and unique ways. It is such a joy to see you both bloom!

To my grandsons, August and Gunny, for teaching me the depth of love that is beyond anything I have experienced. Seeing you both come into this world and watching you grow into your own unique, fierce beings has been one of my greatest joys.

Thank you to my dear soul friends, Gabriela Masala, Misa Hopkins, Sedena Cappannelli, Jenny Hay, Paul Samuel

Dolman, Jacob Liberman, and my amazing, badass meditation teacher Elle Kerr-Wilson for their tremendous love, support, and continued inspiration in my life. Thank you for the depth, joy, and love we share, for believing in me, and for helping me to grow and expand through our connection. I love you all dearly!

A special thank you to my dear friend and mentor Tom Cronin for his beautiful energy, belief in my vision, and for his continued support and guidance that has helped me expand into a greater version of myself. You are a gift to this world.

Deepest heartfelt gratitude to Natalie Ledwell for being an amazing inspiration, total rockstar, and the most fantastic fierce friend to write the forward while she had COVID. Big love and deep appreciation to you!

A heartfelt thank you to Karen Curry Parker, Michelle Vandepas, and GracePoint Publishing for an absolutely phenomenal experience and for believing in this book from its inception. I will forever be thankful to Karen for asking me the fate-filled question, during my interview on her Quantum Revolution podcast, "What's next for you?" which became the opening for this book to be born. Deep thanks to Michelle for our amazing conversation shortly after that, which immediately resulted in the download of the title and outline for this book. You are both amazing women doing such important and valuable work in the world. Thank you for seeing me, valuing my message, and supporting me to bring this passion forth to share with others.

And finally, to my life partner and true love, Morgan Oaks. My deepest love and gratitude for your fierce belief in me, your amazing love, nurturing spirit, and endless hours of laughter (that has kept me up many nights) and has filled my life with tremendous joy. You are the most amazing human being I have ever known and the greatest example of someone who loves the whole world with their entire fierce and wild heart.

ABOUT THE AUTHOR

Stephanie James is a dynamic presenter, author, film producer, transformational coach, and psychotherapist with thirty years in the mental health field. She brings her vision and her passion to all aspects of life. She has gathered wisdom from some of the most amazing minds and serving hearts on the planet and has synthesized their wisdom with her own knowledge and experience to help her audience expand their vision of themselves and ignite their purpose.

She believes her personal purpose is to bring as much love and healing to the world as possible and she understands that when each person lives their greatest version of themselves, they illuminate the way for others to do the same. Each unique light that each person has can make a difference when it is able to shine bright in the world. No matter what challenges she has faced in her life (and there were many), she continues to break through limiting beliefs, opening her heart, and reaching new depths of healing and expansion; continuing to cultivate a truly FIERCE life, full of purpose and passion.

To find out more about Stephanie and connect online, visit StephanieJames.world or scan the code below.

For more great books from Empower Press
Visit Books.GracePointPublishing.com

If you enjoyed reading *Becoming Fierce*, and purchased it through an online retailer, please return to the site and write a review to help others find the book.